THE BATTLE AGAINST BIG TOBACCO

This book made possible by the generosity of:

OSU CENTER FOR HEALTH SCIENCES
UNIVERSITY OF OKLAHOMA HEALTH SCIENCES CENTER

BOB BURKE

JACK ALLEN FAMILY EDUCATION FOUNDATION
EAST CENTRAL UNIVERSITY FOUNDATION
JIM AND CHRISTY EVEREST
CASEY AND HUGH KILLBLANE
SUSAN A. REGIER

THE HEALEY FAMILY
DOUG MATHENY
MARSHALL SNIPES

THE BATTLE AGAINST BIG TOBACCO

AND THE BIRTH OF

TSET

TOBACCO SETTLEMENT ENDOWMENT TRUST

By JULIE BISBEE, MARSHALL SNIPES and BOB BURKE

Foreword by THE HONORABLE DREW EDMONDSON

Series Editor: GINI MOORE CAMPBELL

Printed in Canada
ISBN: 978-1-938923-74-6
Library of Congress Catalog Number: 2025930028
Designed by Julie Rushing

Unless otherwise noted, photographs courtesy of the Tobacco Settlement Endowment Trust (TSET).

Oklahoma acknowledges the traditional and sacred use of tobacco among Native American/American Indian people. In this publication, tobacco refers to the use of commercial tobacco unless otherwise stated.

CONTENTS

ACKNOWLEDGMENTS

We are grateful for the cooperation of many people who made possible this historical perspective of the first quarter century of the Tobacco Settlement Endowment Trust (TSET) in Oklahoma.

The intriguing story of the fight against "Big Tobacco" and the birth and growth of TSET was told in interviews with Hon. William A. "Drew" Edmondson, Doug Matheny, Tracey Strader, Dr. Robert McCaffree, Dr. Robert Mannel, Hon. Robert Butkin, Hon. Jari Askins, Hon. Ben Brown, Hon. Ray Vaughn, Casey Killblane, Kenneth Rowe, Dr. Laura Beebe, Jim Gebhart, Don Millican, Bruce Benjamin, V. Burns Hargis, Hon. Lisa John, Dr. Brad Lieb, Joe Thomas, Hon. Warren Queton, Hon. Frank Keating, Hon. Mike Moore, Hon. Mary Fallin, Hon. Brad Henry, Dr. Kelli Mosteller, Hon. Stratton Taylor, Hon. David Holt, Hon. Ben Robinson, Hon. Loyd Benson, Dr. Donald Cooper, Susan Walters Bize, Terry Cline, and Karla Sneegas.

Our team of proofreaders helped shape the book to final form. They include Thomas Larson, Doug Matheny, Tracey Strader, and Susan Yingling.

The TSET staff, TSET account team at VI Marketing and Branding, and *The Oklahoman* provided photographs that document the positive results of TSET programs and grants. For other photographs, thank you to Trait Thompson and his able staff at the Oklahoma Historical Society, and Linda Linn at *The Oklahoman*.

Excellent editorial comment came from The Chickasaw Nation, including Lisa John, Secretary of Culture & Humanities; Dr. Brad Lieb, director of Chickasaw Archaeology and Field Study; and Joe Thomas, executive officer of Literary Arts. Chickasaw Nation Secretary of Commerce Dan Boren was a conduit for much of the information.

Warren Queton, a Kiowa tribal legislator and adjunct professor in the Department of Native American Studies at the University of Oklahoma, helped us understand the significance of the use of traditional or ceremonial tobacco as opposed to commercial tobacco.

Additional editorial assistance and research came from Tabby Brown and Michelle Douglas. The ultimate guide in writing a book is Gini Moore Campbell, vice president of the Oklahoma Hall of Fame, who has edited more books about Oklahoma than anyone in history.

THE AUTHORS—2025

FOREWORD

The Tobacco Settlement Endowment Trust (TSET) demonstrates how government should work. It exemplifies what can be accomplished if the instruments of government are put in motion to correct a serious problem by creating a funding source and a solution. It shows the wisdom of long-range vision and creative action.

But it started with a lawsuit. I had not run for Attorney General on the issue of tobacco harm. People were enjoying their cigarettes, ignoring the warning labels on the packs, the cigarette companies were making billions, and the States were stuck with medical bills.

I learned of the first such lawsuit in December 1995 at a meeting of attorneys general held in San Diego. It was a meeting that included training for newly elected A.G.'s and an opportunity to meet and listen to Mike Moore, the Mississippi Attorney General, who was already butting heads with his own Governor over his right to sue the tobacco industry.

In the ensuing months we learned through litigation discovery that the tobacco industry referred to children as a "replacement market." They were marketing to kids to replace their older customers who were dying from cancer and other smoking-related illnesses. We learned that industry memos referred to their product as a "nicotine delivery device" because it was the nicotine that was addictive, and the cigarette just supplied the drug.

Linda and Drew Edmondson

Those revelations, and others, opened my eyes and provided the fuel that propelled us into the fight. In 1996 Oklahoma filed suit against big tobacco.

From August to November 1998, the states and the industry met in New York City to hammer out what became the Master Settlement Agreement (MSA). I was one of the attorneys general on the negotiating team. The injunctive relief prevented marketing to children, sponsorship of events including children as participants or as significant numbers of viewers, being untruthful about the health effects of cigarettes, and most forms of advertising. And, there was a revenue stream to the states—more than $200 billion in the first 25 years, over $2 billion of that to Oklahoma.

The question was, "What are we going to do with the money?" I believed the lawsuit was about the health of our citizens and the proceeds should be utilized to meet those needs.

In 1999 work began on a proposed amendment to Oklahoma's Constitution to create a trust to receive the bulk of that money and to require that it be spent primarily on the health of our citizens. State Treasurer Robert Butkin and I chaired that effort. On November 7, 2000, State Question 692 creating the Oklahoma Tobacco Settlement Endowment Trust Fund passed with a "yes" vote of 68.81%.

In this book you will read of the accomplishments made by TSET; their impact on smoking rates, their promotion of healthy lifestyles, their contributions to cancer research, and their work to place doctors in medically deprived sections of the state. This work is a testament to the wisdom of the voters in 2000 and explains the strong support TSET enjoys from Oklahomans today.

DREW EDMONDSON

Drew Edmondson was born in Washington, D.C., where his father, Edmond Augustas "Ed" Edmondson, was later a member of the U.S. House of Representatives from Oklahoma. He graduated from Muskogee High School and Northeastern State University. While in college, he married Linda Larason of Fargo, Oklahoma. He served four years in the U.S. Navy, including a year in Vietnam.

Edmondson was a schoolteacher when he was elected to the Oklahoma House of Representatives. After earning a law degree from The University of Tulsa School of Law, he became an assistant district attorney under Muskogee County District Attorney Michael C. "Mike" Turpen. When Turpen left office to run for Attorney General, Edmondson was elected District Attorney in 1982 and was reelected without opposition in 1986 and 1990.

In 1994, Edmondson was elected Attorney General of Oklahoma. Just two years later, he led Oklahoma to the forefront of the fight against Big Tobacco, first with a lawsuit on behalf of the state, and then as a member of a negotiating team of attorneys general that convinced the tobacco companies to pay the largest settlement in world litigation history. He was Oklahoma Attorney General for 16 years until 2011 and made a generational impact upon the Sooner State.

Drew and Linda have two children. He practices law with the Riggs Abney law firm in Oklahoma City.

INTRODUCTION

By Marshall Snipes, TSET Chairman of the Board
and Julie Bisbee, TSET Executive Director

The creation of Oklahoma's Tobacco Settlement Endowment Trust is a remarkable story of the hard work of a group of advocates, political leaders, and fortuitous foresight in protecting dollars brought to Oklahoma because of the harms inflicted by tobacco use.

Like many southern states, Oklahoma outpaces the rest of the country in number of adult smokers and the disease and death that follows long-term use of tobacco and exposure to second-hand smoke. Oklahoma's laws protecting its citizens are also out-of-step with other states that have lower rates of adult smoking and cancer.

It is clear today, as much as it was 25 years ago, that there are still opportunities for improvement. It is also clear that our policy environment is not void of outside influence and coordinated efforts by the tobacco industry to retain an environment that supports their business model of addiction.

In 1998, as the Master Settlement Agreement was being negotiated, public health advocates in Oklahoma dared to dream big and discuss a way to ensure dollars brought to the state on the backs of citizens could lessen the hold of big tobacco for generations to come. Advocates were fresh from battling for protections against smoking at the Capitol and city halls across the state. They had suffered defeat and were ready to seize the opportunities provided and maximize the potential for funding for tobacco use prevention, reduction, and cessation. Elected officials—Governor Frank Keating, Attorney General Drew Edmondson, State Treasurer Robert Butkin, State Representative Jari Askins—and countless other leaders understood that settlements with industries that have long avoided being held accountable were rare and had the potential to shape the future to come.

And voters agreed and passed a state question to amend the constitution creating the Tobacco Settlement Endowment Trust (TSET) in 2000.

Today, Oklahoma is the only state with a Constitutional endowment that uses the majority of Master Settlement Agreement dollars to fund programs to prevent and reduce tobacco addiction and reduce the leading causes of preventable death in Oklahoma—smoking, poor nutrition, and sedentary lifestyles. As intended, twenty-five years later, annual earnings from the endowment are greater than the annual settlement payments. The tobacco industry will continue to make payments to the states as long as cigarettes are sold.

TSET is something Oklahoma should be proud of. We hope

that by reading about Oklahoma's ongoing effort to reduce the toll of tobacco, TSET continues to reach the high ideals that early creators envisioned. This book also details the ongoing discussion about how to help Oklahomans make healthy choices, and the role of government in those choices.

With five broad areas set forth for endowment earnings, the bi-partisan TSET Board of Directors has consistently focused on making an impact across the state. This foundation was set by its founding board members who developed a strategic focus on prevention and long-term health improvement. This vision is permanently funded; independent of political whims, it is well-positioned for continued success. It is with gratitude to advocates, elected officials, board members, staff, and the public that we celebrate TSET's 25th anniversary and look forward to continued impact.

CHAPTER ONE

AN ANCIENT CROP

The story of tobacco is about how an exotic plant seduced civilization.

— IAIN GATELY

Humans and tobacco have long been associated. Tobacco is derived from the leaves of the genus Nicotiana, a plant from the night-shade family, indigenous to North and South America.

Smoking tobacco most likely evolved from "snuffing," inhaling tobacco powder through the nose. There is other evidence that tobacco was chewed, eaten, smeared over bodies, and used in eye drops. Smoke was offered to the gods and used for controlling insects on crops and fruit trees. Tobacco was believed to be a cure for fever, asthma, gonorrhea, plague, and cancer and was used as a remedy for snake bites.

By the time of the arrival of Christopher Columbus in 1492, tobacco was commonplace in the Americas and even on islands such as Cuba.

Tobacco has played an important role in North American Native American traditions for thousands of years. It is considered a gift from the Creator and is a sacred part of many ceremonies, prayers, and offerings.

"Traditional Tobacco" is naturally grown without the chemicals or processing common with commercial tobacco. Some tribal members grow traditional tobacco in their gardens. The importance of traditional tobacco cannot be overstated. Warren Queton, a Kiowa tribal legislator and adjunct professor in the Department of Native American Studies at the University of Oklahoma, said:

> My uncle, Daniel Cozad, Sr., always says, "This tobacco is key to heaven, that's how we believe and talk to God!" This underscores the belief that when used correctly, traditional tobacco is a conduit for our prayers to the Creator. Its role in prayer and spiritual practice is profound and it is not something to be taken lightly.

Traditional tobacco is used in various sacred practices such as pipe ceremonies and offering rituals. The Kiowas place tobacco in the earth as an offering when harvesting sage, cedar, sweetgrass, or after killing a deer or buffalo. Queton said, "In the Native American Church, we roll tobacco in a corn husk to create a natural cigarette, instead of a pipe, which is then used in prayer ceremonies." Among the Seminole Nation of Oklahoma, traditional tobacco is considered a sacred medicine. It is commonly used for prayer or spiritual protection or to express thanks to someone.

The Citizen Potawatomi Nation has been successful in cultivating and processing traditional *séma* or tobacco for use in medicine and sacred ceremonies. *Courtesy Citizen Potawatomi Nation.*

Chickasaw and other Southeastern Indian tribes used pipes made of materials such as stone or clay for smoking traditional tobacco. Dr. Brad Lieb, Director of Archaeology and Field Study of The Chickasaw Nation, said, "Tribal archaeologists reveal they smoked tobacco during council or important meetings, during ceremony, and also for pleasure."

Dr. Kelli Mosteller is an enrolled citizen of the Citizen Potawatomi Nation and CEO of Oklahoma City's First Americans Museum. Several tribal nations, including the Citizen Potawatomi, have refined methods to enable citizens to raise their own sacred tobacco. She said:

> We are now able to see the full life cycle of the tobacco plant, from tiny seeds, germination, planting, and finally, harvesting and processing, as a community. This includes drying the leaves for smoking and other ceremonial uses. At each stage of the life cycle, we pray and tend the plants, knowing that the very act of caring for them is itself a part of the ceremony.

Cigarettes were first made by hand, either by the smoker or in small factories. Philip Morris opened its first shop in England in 1847, selling hand-rolled Turkish cigarettes. The first cigarette rolling machine was invented in 1880.

The arrival of cigarette-making machines made the production of cigarettes cheaper and faster. Soon, cigarettes became the preferred method of smoking tobacco. With lower production costs, the price of cigarettes was within reach to people of all income levels.

In the latter years of the 19th century, cigarettes became a symbol of modern culture. Cigarette smoking became a fashionable trend among young people and women as traditional gender roles were challenged by smoking in public.

The American military encouraged smoking in the early 20th century. During World War I, cigarettes were a staple for soldiers. Tobacco companies sent free samples to soldiers fighting on the front line. Tobacco became a global commodity with manufacturers developing new products and targeting different demographics to expand their customer base.

It was during this time that American tobacco companies ramped up their marketing and advertising campaigns. They hired doctors and dentists in the 1940s to endorse their products and reduce public health concerns about the risks of smoking. Advertisements used misleading slogans such as "Just What the Doctor Ordered" and "More Doctors Smoke Camels" to convince smokers that their health would not be affected by smoking.

Movie stars and athletes were hired to endorse a particular brand of cigarette. Tobacco companies bought and sponsored

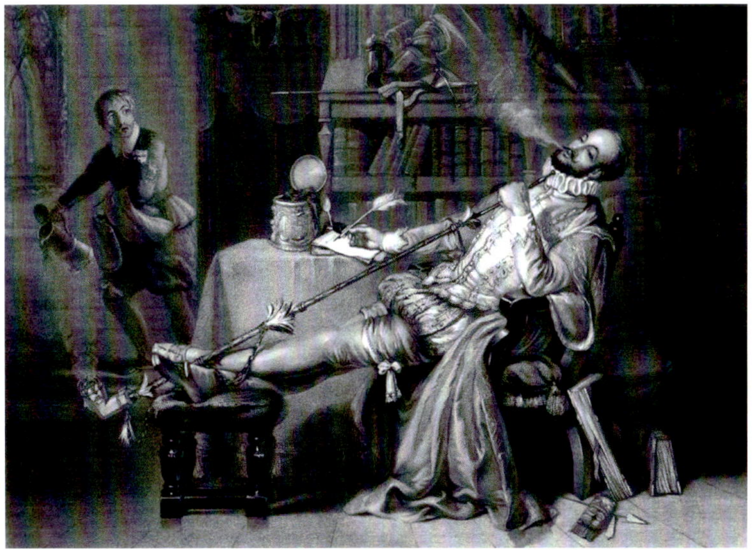

Sir Walter Raleigh using a long clay pipe to smoke tobacco. *Courtesy Fairlynch Museum.*

Tobacco leaves drying. *Courtesy National Archives.*

A Lucky Strike ad promoted a richer, more glamorous life through smoking. *Courtesy Modern Graphic History Library, Washington University Libraries.*

Cigarette company ads targeted women.

the most popular television programs. Cultural icons, such as the Marlboro Man, lured men to smoke with fantasies of manliness and independence. The smoking advertising and promotion was unprecedented on a national scale.

Author Iain Gately wrote:

> Propelled to fame by an immense advertising budget, Marlboro Man began to ride nightly across American TV screens in 1964. He lived in a giant, scenic landscape named "Marlboro Country," and viewers' hearts leaped as the beauties of their own fair land were revealed. Marlboro Man did not look like he would ultimately succumb to lung cancer.

A Marlboro cigarette ad. By 1972, Marlboro was the best-selling brand in the world. *Courtesy Modern Graphic History Library, Washington University Libraries.*

Actor and future President Ronald Reagan endorsed cigarettes before the health hazards were widely known. President Reagan later said he regretted his endorsement. *Courtesy Modern Graphic History Library, Washington University Libraries.*

In 1960, 42% of adult Americans smoked cigarettes. *Courtesy Modern Graphic History Library, Washington University Libraries.*

Cigarette smoking crossed ethnic, socioeconomic, gender, and racial boundaries. By the 1960s, 42% of adult Americans smoked. The average U.S. adult smoked more than 7,000 cigarettes per year. Most men, 53%, and about one-third of the country's women were regular smokers. Smoking was allowed in public spaces such as hospitals, airplanes, and restaurants.

The tobacco industry had a powerful influence on Congress and the legislatures of many states, especially in southern states where the tobacco industry flourished. Oklahoma was one of the states where tobacco company lobbyists were well received by legislators.

CHAPTER TWO

EARLY CONCERNS

There has never been a product that is both loved and hated as much, or by so many people, as the cigarette. There are those who exalt its pleasures, while others consider it evil and crusade to eliminate its use and existence.

— JORGE LUIS ARMENTEROS

The anti-smoking movement is not new. In England, King James I anonymously wrote a tract that argued that tobacco use was immoral and irresponsible, like drunkenness, had negative health effects, was religiously offensive, and was a habit of low prestige.

Smoking is hateful to the nose, harmful to the brain, and dangerous to the lungs.

— KING JAMES I

However, by the end of the 17th century, the lure of profit gained in trading tobacco overrode any attempts in England and other European countries to ban or regulate tobacco. The English colonies were heavily dependent on growing tobacco.

After the United States gained independence, pipe smoking and snuff were popular. Only when chewing tobacco and cigar smoking grew in prominence in the late 19th century did reformers take notice. Reformers viewed tobacco use as a moral issue. Little attention was paid to the health effects of tobacco. Instead, smoking by young boys was often the focus of the anti-cigarette movement that was modeled after the temperance movement by religious groups to reduce alcohol consumption.

Prior to 1950, studies on smoking and lung cancer reported conflicting results. Many newspaper editors refused to publish the reports for fear of offending tobacco companies that advertised heavily in the media.

Physicians did not generally see a significant health threat for most smokers. To combat the inconclusive studies, the cigarette companies made claims that harmful corrosive acids were removed, and cigarette smoking could improve health. Camel advertised "Smoking Camels stimulates the natural flow of digestive fluids . . . and increases alkalinity." Kool menthol cigarettes were handed out to patients by nose and throat specialists to help with colds.

American scholars and activists were aware of increasing cancer death rates. Statisticians in the insurance industry documented the growing influence of cancer as cigarette smoking swept the country.

The breakthrough came when the research of British epidemiologist Richard Doll and his fellow researcher, Austin Bradford Hill, was published in the *British Medical Journal* in 1950. The findings concluded:

> The risk of developing [lung cancer] increases in proportion to the amount smoked. It may be 50 times as great among those who smoke 25 or more cigarettes a day as among non-smokers.

Doll and Hill studied lung cancer patients in 20 London hospitals. At first, they believed automobile exhaust was at fault, but quickly discovered tobacco smoking was the only common factor. Doll himself stopped smoking because of his findings.

In 1954, a study by 40,000 British doctors came to the same conclusion as Doll and Hill, prompting the government of the United Kingdom to advise its citizens of a link between smoking and lung cancer.

At the middle of the 20th century, evidence showing a direct connection between cigarette smoking and lung cancer was mounting. The analysis by researchers revealed:

- Cigarette smoke contains more than 4,000 chemicals and many of these are harmful. Primary tobacco biohazardous compounds include at least 43 carcinogens, such as nicotine and nitrosamines. Tobacco smoke contains herbicide, fungicide, pesticide residues, and tars.
- When smoking, the harmful chemicals enter one's lungs and affect the entire body.
- Chemicals in cigarette smoke also make it harder for our cells to repair damage. This means damage can build up.
- It is the buildup of damage in the same cell over time that leads to cancer.

In the United States, there was widespread concern about the long-term effects of cigarette smoking. However, the sheer power of the tobacco industry held back any authoritative government action.

Executives of the major tobacco companies met in December 1953 and devised a unified strategy to answer growing research studies. They formed the Tobacco Industry Research Committee. A leading researcher was hired to publicly assume a position of skepticism. In a strategy that continued for decades, the industry denied the harm of its products, discredited scientific evidence that linked smoking to lung cancer, and funded research to divert attention from cigarettes. In addition, they marketed new products with implied lower risks than old fashioned cigarettes.

The Tobacco Institute was created by tobacco companies in 1958 as a trade association to put out good news about tobacco, especially economic news, and rebut studies that showed tobacco use was harmful. The Master Settlement Agreement (MSA) in 1998 disbanded the Institute.

In 1960, John F. Kennedy was elected President of the United States. The American Heart Association, the American Cancer Society, the National Tuberculosis Association, now the American Lung Association, and the American Public Health Association persuaded President Kennedy to name an expert study committee to advise Surgeon General Luther L. Terry on the health effects of smoking. The associations, led by some of the most prominent physicians in the American medical community, believed that unrestricted tobacco advertising took advantage of those who were the most vulnerable—the young and the poor.

The 1964 *Surgeon General's Report on Smoking and Health* was transformative in the war against Big Tobacco in the United States. Its bold conclusion was:

U.S. Surgeon General Luther L. Terry, himself a longtime smoker, released his anti-smoking report on January 11, 1964, in a dramatic, nationally televised press conference. Two hundred reporters were present and were allowed to study a copy of the report before asking questions. The report received enormous publicity. *Newsweek* Magazine called it "monumental." *Courtesy National Library of Medicine.*

> Cigarette smoking is causally related to lung cancer; the magnitude of the effect of cigarette smoking far outweighs all other factors. In comparison with nonsmokers, average male smokers of cigarettes have approximately a nine to tenfold risk of developing lung cancer and heavy smokers at least a twenty-fold risk.

It was difficult for physicians to argue with the Surgeon General's focus on methodology and analysis of case studies. Also, the prestige of the members of the Advisory Committee was heralded as creating a panel that was unbiased in its approach to a growing national health problem.

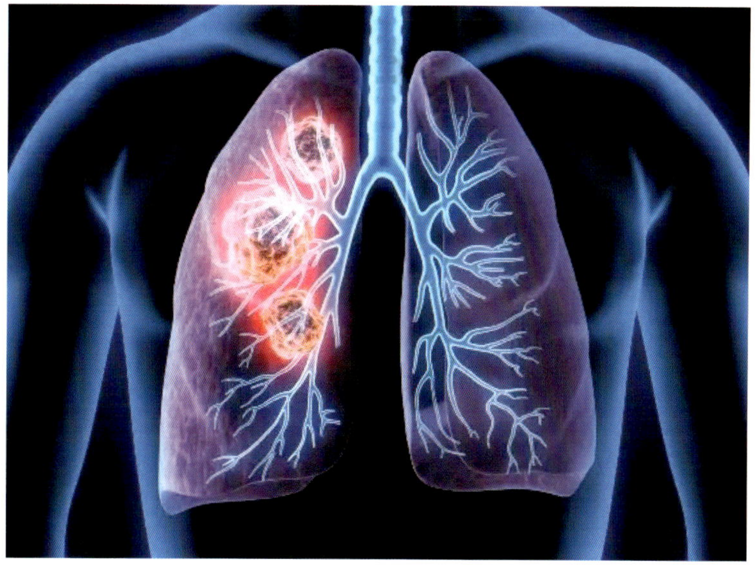

A graphic description of the attack of cancer upon the lungs. Lung cancer forms in the tissues of the lung, usually in the cells that line the air passages. It is the leading cause of cancer death in both men and women. There are two main types: small cell lung cancer and non-small cell lung cancer. *Courtesy Centers for Disease Control and Prevention (CDC).*

The conclusions reached by the report were arguably the most important and far-reaching in the history of public health and constituted a classic example of science driving public policy. It gave extraordinary momentum to the tobacco control movement and caused public opinion and behavior to change considerably, even though a large part of the population was not initially predisposed to accept the message.

The Surgeon General's report said the health hazard was of sufficient importance to warrant appropriate remedial action. But it was unclear what the government could do. Realizing that tobacco products were legal, the federal government decided that all it could do was to advise consumers of the hazards involved.

Dr. Albert Rizzo, chief medical officer of the American Lung Association, said:

> This report alerted the nation, really for the first time, to the health risks of smoking and it transformed the issue from one of just individual and consumer choice to really one of epidemiology, public health, and risk for smokers and nonsmokers alike.

As a response to the Surgeon General's report, Congress enacted the Federal Cigarette Labeling and Advertising Act of 1965 mandating the first warning to appear on cigarette packages:

Caution:
Cigarette Smoking May Be Hazardous to Your Health.

A study published later by the National Institutes of Health, said, "Subsequent analyses have shown how the tobacco industry used its connections within government to assure a weak bill and a weak warning label." It was pointed out that the words "may be hazardous" was in sharp contrast with the findings of the Surgeon General's report that "cigarette smoking is causally related to lung cancer."

Subsequent government actions focused on promoting campaigns to inform the public about the risks of cigarette smoking and how the risks might be reduced. The Surgeon General convened another group of experts in 1966 to develop recommendations for reducing the tar and nicotine content of cigarette smoke.

At about the same time, the Federal Trade Commission (FTC) revised its advertising rules to allow manufacturers to include in ads "a factual statement of the tar and nicotine content of the mainstream smoke from a cigarette." The federal government, through the National Clearinghouse for Smoking and Health,

THE IMPACT ON FUTURE DOCTORS

The Surgeon General's report of 1964 impacted medical students. A Harvard University professor later wrote:

> At the time, I was a first-year medical student. Between two thirds and three quarters of my fellow students were smokers. By the time we graduated, only 10% remained smokers. The report was one big reason why.
>
> The impact of the report was augmented by our experience dissecting cadavers. The lungs of non-smokers were pink. The lungs of heavy smokers were black. That didn't look healthy, and the surgeon general confirmed that it wasn't.

produced a pamphlet aimed at people who did not want to quit smoking but wanted to reduce their risk. The pamphlet had five suggestions:

- Choose a cigarette with less tar and nicotine
- Don't smoke the entire cigarette
- Take fewer draws
- Reduce inhaling, and
- Smoke fewer cigarettes.

Even after the 1964 Surgeon General's report, there was not a dramatic change in public beliefs about smoking. A Harris Poll in 1966 found that only 40% of those questioned recognized smoking as a major cause of lung cancer. Another 27% considered it a minor cause and one-third of those surveyed said science had not yet proven a relationship between smoking and lung cancer.

After advertising of cigarettes on radio and television was banned in 1971, tobacco companies ramped up advertising in magazines and on outdoor billboards. Even though many individual doctors rapidly accepted the findings, the American Medical Association (AMA) took more than two decades to take a clear stand on the health impacts of smoking. The AMA opposed Medicare and proposed national health insurance. They needed the support from congressional allies in southern tobacco-growing states for that policy stance.

Joseph A. Califano, Jr., became Secretary of the Department of Health, Education, and Welfare (HEW) in the administration of President Jimmy Carter, and laid out a battle plan for a vigorous anti-smoking campaign. He called cigarette smoking "Public Health Enemy Number One" and "slow motion suicide." He launched a major public information and education effort against smoking. Califano's message was that lung cancer from smoking was not just a problem for the smoker—it was a drag on nonsmokers because of the spiraling costs of medical care and tax increases necessary for treatment of tobacco-related cancer.

Another significant landmark was the 1986 Surgeon General's report. For the first time, the report concluded that secondhand smoke could cause lung cancer in healthy adult nonsmokers and respiratory symptoms in children. The report released substantial evidence from researchers worldwide. Surgeon General C. Everett Koop was an outspoken foe of tobacco.

Meanwhile, tobacco companies targeted studies that exposed the unhealthy result of secondhand smoke. Research was commissioned to undermine the scientific findings. Major tobacco companies purchased newspaper ads that discredited the conclusions.

Dr. C. Everett Koop was chosen by President Ronald Reagan as Surgeon General. Koop was blunt in his attacks on Big Tobacco.

> *The right of smokers to smoke ends where their behavior affects the health and well-being of others.*
>
> — SURGEON GENERAL C. EVERETT KOOP

Between 1985-1988, more than 300 cities across the country enacted laws restricting public smoking. In 1988, Congress banned smoking on all U.S. domestic flights of less than two hours. Later, the ban was extended to ban smoking on all domestic flights.

The 1988 Surgeon General's report changed the view that smoking was just a habit. The report said nicotine caused addiction and compared it to other addicting drugs, including heroin and cocaine. The findings contradicted the argument that people became smokers by their own free choice.

Research showed the level of nicotine in the brain is crucial for the highly dependent smoker as 20-30 minutes after completing a cigarette, nicotine had left the brain for other organs. That was about the time the dependent smoker needed another cigarette. The smoker was hooked.

By the 1980s, the social norms around smoking changed from acceptance and woven into the daily lives of Americans to the increasing unacceptability of smoking due to an increased public understanding of the dangers of cigarettes. Local and state groups of nonsmokers demanded smoke-free environments.

CHAPTER THREE

CONGRESSIONAL HEARINGS

From the foundation of the nation, Congress used its constitutional power to enter the public health arena. In 1798, Congress authorized the formation of the U.S. Marine Hospital Service, the forerunner of the U.S. Public Health Service. National disease monitoring was first conducted in 1850.

In 1938, Congress passed the Federal Food, Drug, and Cosmetic Act, requiring manufacturers to provide scientific proof of a new drug's safety. In 1953, President Dwight D. Eisenhower created the U.S. Department of Health, Education, and Welfare (HEW). In 1979, responsibility for health was transferred to the new Department of Health and Human Services (HHS).

In the later years of the 20th century, the growth of scientific knowledge around disease reduction and control and public acceptance of the practice created an atmosphere in which public health became a public responsibility.

With the federal government's increasing role in the anti-smoking campaign, it was natural for Congress to hold public hearings. A young congressman from California began waging a 25-year anti-tobacco effort. Henry Waxman, a Los Angeles lawyer and grandson of Jewish immigrants from Russia, was elected to the U.S. House of Representatives in 1974 and was re-elected 17 times without significant opposition.

In 1979, Waxman became chairman of the House Committee on Energy and Commerce's Subcommittee on Health and the Environment. In 1982, he held the first congressional hearing on the health risks of smoking. Two years later, he engineered a bipartisan effort to require cigarette packages to contain one of four warnings, rotated quarterly:

- SURGEON GENERAL'S WARNING: Smoking Causes Lung Cancer, Heart Disease, Emphysema, and May Complicate Pregnancy
- SURGEON GENERAL'S WARNING: Smoking by Pregnant Women May Result in Fetal Injury, Premature Birth, and Low Birth Weight
- SURGEON GENERAL'S WARNING: Cigarette Smoke Contains Carbon Monoxide
- SURGEON GENERAL'S WARNING: Quitting Smoking Now Greatly Reduces Serious Risks to Your Health.

In 1985, Waxman held a hearing on the effects of smokeless tobacco products such as chewing tobacco and snuff. He said, "Smokeless

Congressman Henry Waxman spearheaded congressional oversight to expose the health hazards of tobacco. When he retired in 2014, Matthew Myers, the president of the Campaign for Tobacco-Free Kids, wrote about Waxman, "When no one else in Congress dared to take on Big Tobacco, he conducted scores of hearings. . . . America owes Henry Waxman a profound debt."

Courtesy Centers for Disease Control and Prevention (CDC).

tobacco is not, as its advertising suggests, a safe alternative to cigarettes." The following year, he led a successful bi-partisan effort with Republican U.S. Senator Richard Lugar of Indiana to require health warnings on smokeless tobacco products and to ban advertisements of smokeless tobacco on radio and television. Throughout the 1980s and early 1990s, the anti-smoking legislation in Congress was made possible by cooperation between Republicans and Democrats.

Food and Drug Administration (FDA) Commissioner David Kessler announced evidence in February 1994 that tobacco manufacturers were deliberately manipulating the nicotine content in cigarettes and the FDA was prepared to consider regulating tobacco products. A month later, Waxman's subcommittee invited Kessler to testify. The testimony was dramatic, detailing ways in which tobacco companies had manipulated their products to increase addiction. An R.J. Reynolds Tobacco Company patent to more than double nicotine levels in its tobacco blends was made public.

Waxman publicly announced that his subcommittee would invite the CEOs of the country's seven largest tobacco companies to appear at the next hearing, and they would be the only witnesses. The announcement caught the attention of the national media.

On April 14, 1994, the top officials of each of the companies appeared. The opening statement by Waxman was compelling. The following are excerpts:

> No health issue is as important as cigarette smoking. . . . The truth is that cigarettes are the single most dangerous consumer product ever sold. Nearly a half-million Americans die every year as a result of tobacco. . . . Imagine our Nation's outrage if two fully loaded jumbo jets crashed each day, killing all aboard. Yet that is the same number of Americans that cigarettes kill every 24 hours.
>
> This hearing marks the beginning of a new relationship between Congress and the tobacco companies. The old rules are out, the standards that apply to every other company are in.
>
> An old proverb says that a journey of a thousand miles must begin with a single step. Today is the first step. Many

The heads of the seven largest American tobacco companies are sworn to tell the truth in their appearance at an April 14, 1994, hearing of a U.S. House subcommittee chaired by Congressman Henry Waxman. Each of the tobacco company executives testified that nicotine was not addictive, contrary to what most Americans believed, and what overwhelming research showed. *Courtesy National Archives.*

more are to come as we deal with the most serious health problem facing our Nation.

The tobacco company executives were sworn in. During the seven-hour hearing shown live on CNN and C-Span, they testified they did not believe nicotine was addictive, they denied using advertising such as cartoon characters like Joe Camel to target children, and they disagreed with the Surgeon General's and the American Medical Association's estimate that 400,000 Americans died from smoking-related illnesses each year. However, all admitted they preferred that their own children not smoke. They also admitted that their products, especially the low-tar brands, did use high-nicotine blends of tobacco to deliver more nicotine to the smoker. They insisted the extra nicotine was for flavor.

Oklahoma Congressman Mike Synar asked the Philip Morris CEO if his company had refused to allow one of its own researchers to release a paper describing animal studies that demonstrated the addictiveness of nicotine. The CEO admitted that the paper had twice been hushed.

Synar and Chairman Waxman pressed the tobacco company leaders to supply to Congress many private company papers, including research on humans and animals related to nicotine and addiction. The CEOs had no real choice but to agree.

When Philip Morris CEO William Campbell said all products, from soft drinks to Twinkies, had risks associated with them, Waxman said, "Yes, but the difference between cigarettes and Twinkies is death."

Andrew H. Tisch, chairman of Lorillard Tobacco Company, was asked if he knew cigarettes caused cancer. He replied, "I do not believe that." Waxman asked, "Do you understand how isolated you are from the scientific community in your belief?" Tisch said, "I do, sir."

Oklahoma Congressman Mike Synar was a leader of the congressional anti-smoking effort. He was elected from Oklahoma's Second Congressional District at the age of 28. He served eight terms in Congress and died in 1996 of a brain tumor at the age of 45. *Courtesy Cable-Satellite Public Affairs Network (C-SPAN)*

To repair their public image, all new CEOs of the nation's largest tobacco companies appeared before Congress in 1998. Embarrassing internal industry documents had been released that showed R.J. Reynolds targeted teenagers with its marketing. The head of RJR Nabisco, the parent company of Reynolds, said, "I believe it is immoral . . . unethical, as well as illegal to market to people underage." Tobacco company leaders acknowledged for the first time in a public forum that smoking played a role in lung cancer. A report in *The Washington Post* summarized the hearing:

> Chief executives of the once-defiant tobacco industry came before Congress yesterday contrite and conciliatory and made their strongest public admissions ever that smoking is hazardous and addictive.

The tobacco industry's problems were far from over. The focus of the anti-smoking campaign had shifted to the legislatures and courtrooms in several states, including Oklahoma.

CHAPTER FOUR

CHANGING THE CULTURE IN OKLAHOMA

Nonsmokers objected to smokers lighting up in public. Some did not like the smell of cigarette smoke, while others were sensitive or allergic to the smoke.

For more than 25 years in Oklahoma, the culture around tobacco had been changing. Oklahomans were concerned, but before science proved the link between cigarette smoke and lung cancer and other diseases, the objection to smoking was based upon religious and moral grounds. Some church groups believed smoking was a sin.

In 1964, Dr. Herschel Hobbs, pastor of Oklahoma City's First Baptist Church, called smoking a "sin against the body." He said, "We can only imply from references in the Bible as to the care of the body, that smoking is not to be encouraged."

Even though it would be decades before tobacco companies would be held liable for the deaths of Americans, Oklahoma City attorney Robert Grove filed a lawsuit against a dozen tobacco companies in 1961. Grove represented Hazel Shields of Holdenville, Oklahoma, whose husband, Ed, died in 1958 after

University of Oklahoma football fans who took a special train from Oklahoma City to Norman for games convinced the Santa Fe Railroad to set aside two non-smoking cars in 1949. *Courtesy Oklahoma Historical Society.*

smoking three packs a day for 30 years. Unfortunately, Oklahoma County District Judge A.P. VanMeter dismissed the case in April 1961, stating it was impossible to prove the actions of the tobacco companies caused Ed Shields' death.

In 1963, longtime Oklahoma City newspaperwoman Katherine Hatch surveyed Oklahoma's colleges and high schools about cigarette smoking. She found rules to be liberal. Senior high schools generally had an outdoor area designated for smoking students and teachers and allowed smoking at sporting events and in teachers' lounges.

At the state's largest public universities, students were allowed to smoke in larger classrooms. Bethany Nazarene College and Phillips University in Enid did not allow smoking anywhere on campus. At Oklahoma Christian College and Oklahoma Baptist University, men were allowed to smoke at certain places, but women were not allowed to smoke at all. Central State College in Edmond, The University of Tulsa, Panhandle A&M College in Goodwell, and Northeastern State College in Tahlequah enforced a no-smoking ban in classrooms.

When Surgeon General Luther L. Terry released the 1964 report linking cigarette smoking to heart disease, lung cancer, and bronchial complaints, Oklahomans were quick to respond. The Oklahoma Chapter of the American Cancer Society offered programs and brochures to help smokers. Ross McLennan, executive secretary of Sooner Alcohol-Narcotics Education (SANE), asked Oklahoma's congressional delegation to sponsor a bill to ban all tobacco advertising. McLennan said:

> The general public health is involved, and the public welfare should not be placed in jeopardy by any pressure from the tobacco industry.

Roy P. Stewart, a columnist for *The Daily Oklahoman*, the state's largest newspaper, wrote:

> The federal report merely adds research emphasis to something we've really known all the time. The *Reader's Digest* crusading and similar scare stories of recent years sort of took the fun out of cigarette smoking for many people. The sales curve always went back up though. No sensible person will make much of a case for any tobacco use.

A 1964 poll sponsored by the Oklahoma Tuberculosis Association, later called the Oklahoma Chapter of the American Lung Association, found that educational programs needed to start when children were young. In Tulsa, 12% of boys and 5% of girls were smoking in the seventh grade. The parental example played a role in the results of the survey. If neither parent smoked, the percentage of their children with the habit was low. The Tulsa pollsters found that mothers played the most significant role in contributing to children's smoking. More youngsters smoked if their mothers did.

A positive result of the Surgeon General's report in Oklahoma was the action by many local school boards to mandate teachers in science classes to present projects demonstrating the harm cigarettes could do. Some educators believed anti-smoking information should be provided to first graders.

Smoking cessation and products to reduce the harm of smoking were introduced in the 1960s and 1970s. Local newspapers contained ads about Bantron, a small white pill that was touted to help four of five smokers quit. The Aquafilter Pacific Corporation of California promoted and sold a tiny, inconspicuous, pre-moistened filter-holder for a cigarette. Ads claimed 84% of tar was eliminated by using the filter.

Other cigarette "smoker's kits" were popular at natural and health food stores in Oklahoma. At an Oklahoma City store, Tauscher's, a smoker's kit consisting of a cigarette holder and "kickers," were sold. It was promised that by the time the kit was used, "the desire for nicotine is gone."

Several filter-manufacturing companies began selling home air filter systems. Universal Dynamic, Inc., an Oklahoma City firm, promised in a 1973 newspaper ad that its air filter system would remove up to 99% of harmful cigarette smoke from a home or business.

Despite the warnings and educational efforts, Oklahomans were smoking at a higher rate in 1971 than the year before. The Tobacco Tax Council reported that 26.7 million cigarettes were purchased in Oklahoma in August 1971 and state tax coffers were sweetened to the tune of $3.4 million.

CHAPTER FIVE

THE TOBACCO LOBBY TAKES CHARGE

The tobacco companies were well-practiced at hiring well-connected lobbyists . . . and hiding behind "third-party" allies to stay out of the public eye and manipulating the process in Oklahoma to kill effective tobacco control policies despite strong public support for those measures.

— STANTON A. GLANTZ, IN FOREWORD TO *HEARTLAND TOBACCO WAR*

Since 1967, tobacco companies and their trade associations have successfully interfered with lawmaking in Oklahoma. If the industry could not defeat an entire bill, they successfully weakened any measure, often behind closed doors in the closing days of a legislative session.

An example was the industry's defeat of House Bill 666 in 1967 that provided for the creation of a full-time Smoking & Health Program Director at the Oklahoma State Department of Health (OSDH). An internal tobacco industry memo discovered during later lawsuits confirmed the involvement of tobacco lobbyists in killing the 1967 bill:

> Current status: Killed in Committee.
> Comment: We were active in opposition of this bill.

Money was no barrier for the tobacco industry to hire the best lobbyists. William A. "Bill" Reynolds was the lobbyist for the Tobacco Tax Council in the 1970s before being hired by the Tobacco Institute. Reynolds was a veteran of Oklahoma Democratic politics and was effective with older, powerful members of the legislature. Later, Big Tobacco supplemented Reynolds' efforts and retained the services of former legislator Kenneth R. Nance who would successfully represent the industry to thwart anti-smoking measures for two decades.

Many cities and towns promoted efforts to protect their citizens from tobacco use and smoke. The efforts of the tobacco industry to minimize changes at the state level were well known, but the industry also invested heavily to erode local power.

Cities such as Norman struggled to enact anti-smoking ordinances. During a November 1973 council meeting, City Attorney Fielding Haas lit a cigarette during discussion to show his opposition to any ban on smoking during city council meetings or in businesses. On the other hand, non-smoking Fire Chief Gene Akin was against all smoking and favored an ordinance to ban cigarette smoking in any place where highly combustible materials were handled. After putting off a vote on an ordinance, the matter was dead.

Industry leaders had a scripted procedure for dealing with cities, towns, and counties. The R.J. Reynolds *Political Action Guide*, distributed to trade associations of pro tobacco businesses, said:

> Often, when an anti-tobacco threat comes up at the local level, your city council or county supervisors will hold hearings to gather public input on the issue. You and your business associates should be sure to attend. Better yet, arrange to testify against the unfair proposal. Through such public testimony, business leaders have often headed off proposed smoking bans and cigarette sales restrictions . . .
>
> They've spoken out boldly, describing how the proposal would hurt local business. And they've made a dramatic impact.

Tobacco companies increased advertising budgets all over the world, including in Oklahoma. Local newspaper ads by the makers of Vantage proclaimed, "Vantage is not the lowest tar and nicotine cigarette. But it is the lowest tar and nicotine cigarette you'll enjoy smoking." A 1972 ad stated, "Anyone who's old enough to smoke is old enough to make up his own mind."

The Oklahoma Chapter of the American Heart Association began a program in 1973 to focus on the hazards to pregnant women who smoked. They cited statistics that one in three expectant mothers were smokers. Dr. Alice Gambill, chair of the community service committee of the American Heart Association, warned that women who smoked during pregnancy had more premature babies than nonsmoking mothers-to-be.

The Oklahoma State Department of Health (OSDH) declared in 1976 that cigarette smoking was the number one drug abuse problem in public schools. *Courtesy Oklahoma Historical Society.*

Anti-smoking groups often banded together to promote cessation workshops. The Oklahoma Interagency Council on Smoking and Health sponsored workshops in 1973 in El Reno, Tulsa, Altus, Lawton, McAlester, and Midwest City. W. Kenneth "Ken" Bonds, a Baptist Hospital official, was chairman of the coordinating agency. He said, "Small, well-directed programs like this have a better chance of getting people to stop smoking." Participants attended two evening sessions per week for a month.

By January 1974, a decade after the Surgeon General's report, cigarette sales were at an all-time high in the United States. Ten million Americans had quit smoking, but a steady influx of new smokers increased the ranks of current smokers from 50 million in 1964 to 52 million in 1974. Data showed no significant drop in smoking among teenagers. In fact, new reports showed that youngsters were beginning to smoke at earlier ages, and there was a dramatic increase in the percentage of girls who smoked.

During the 1974 Oklahoma legislative session, a move to ban smoking in public places never got off the ground. The best that could be done was a legislative resolution calling for a study of controls on smokers and tobacco advertising. State Representative Victor Wickersham of Mangum, a non-smoker, and 41 other smoking and non-smoking House members introduced House Concurrent Resolution 1110. Wickersham said, "It seems only natural to establish guidelines for separate smoking areas in both public places and public modes of transportation."

Another state group, the Oklahoma Coalition for Clean Air, descended upon the State Capitol in October 1974 to support a smoking ban in public places. The coalition was made up of volunteers for anti-smoking organizations and doctors who encouraged their patients to immediately stop smoking, for their own sake and for the good health of their families and coworkers.

In 1975, the first anti-smoking bill gained traction in the Oklahoma legislature. Representative George Camp, an Oklahoma City Republican, argued for the bill on the House floor as some of his colleagues faked coughing. Camp's bill was written to prohibit cigarette or cigar smoking in elevators, indoor movie theaters, libraries, art galleries, concert halls, skating rinks, museums, and buses. Representative Bob Parris of Sallisaw sought to amend the bill to ban smoking in automobiles. His effort failed.

The State Senate added restaurants to the smoking ban bill. That nearly killed the measure. The Oklahoma Restaurant Association reported restaurant owners from around the state complained a ban on smoking would cost them customers. The Senate amendment mandated that the main dining area of any restaurant must be designated for use only by nonsmokers.

Cooper Lyon, owner of Oklahoma City's Anna Maude Cafeteria, was against the inclusion of restaurants. He said, "If they're not permitted to smoke in my cafeteria, then customers will go to a private club where they can smoke and eat."

Recognizing that the Senate amendment threatened making any progress on the issue, Representative Camp asked the House to reject the Senate amendment adding restaurants to the ban. The House followed his suggestion. House Bill 1009 was then passed by both houses and sent to Governor David L. Boren. When the law went into effect in September 1975, it became a misdemeanor with a maximum fine of $100.

A year later, not one violator of the state ban on smoking in certain public spaces had been prosecuted. However, Oklahoma County Assistant District Attorney Mark Blasdel, said it was a good law and there had been no need for prosecution because many smokers, as a matter of personal courtesy, were smoking elsewhere. Blasdel said if he did receive a complaint, he would first talk to the smoker before filing charges.

Smoking bans were opposed by many businesses and civic leaders. On the morning of November 22, 1977, the city council in Oklahoma City passed a smoking ban in city-owned facilities such as the State Fair Arena, Myriad Convention Center, and city meeting rooms. When the Oklahoma City Chamber of Commerce heard the news, the chamber's general manager, Harry Birdwell, rushed to City Hall to ask the council to rescind the ban because of the harm it would do to the National Finals Rodeo held each year at the State Fairgrounds Arena.

Birdwell said a smoking ban would insult the R.J. Reynolds and Winston tobacco companies that provided prize money and advertising for the rodeo. Chamber official Stanley Draper, Jr., agreed. The city council rescinded the ban the same day it was passed, referring the matter to their Planning Committee. The proposed ordinance was ultimately defeated. Even without the smoking ban, Oklahoma City was only able to keep the National Finals through 1978 when it moved to Las Vegas.

Internal tobacco industry memos showed how lobbyists, with the help of business representatives, killed the ordinance:

> On Tuesday of this week, the ordinance came up for final hearing, all our "troops" were there. . . . As you will recall, this is the second measure killed in Oklahoma this year . . . our success has been everyone working together. Please pass my thanks to the companies for the large turnout of their representatives. It really has helped!

Even though the scientific community presented increasing evidence of the danger of secondhand smoke, the Tobacco Institute wrote a letter to Oklahoma City Mayor Patience Latting and members of the city council that provided cover for the defeat of the proposed anti-smoking ordinance:

> It is our belief that tobacco smoke constitutes no health hazard to non-smokers in public places and that there is no convincing evidence to support such a claim. It is respectfully submitted that neither City Ordinances or State Statutes can legislate good manners to inconsiderate smokers.

Doug Bowman, 18, Putnam City High School senior, left, and Christy Hayes, 9, Edmond, display two of the winning posters in the Health Hazards of Smoking Poster Contest sponsored by the Oklahoma Lung Association in 1980. *Courtesy Oklahoma Historical Society.*

In 1979, the Oklahoma Chapter of the American Lung Association sent a letter to the principal of every public and private school in Oklahoma urging the ban of cigarette smoking on school property. School administrators believed the ban was a good idea but would be impossible to enforce. At least one school, Putnam City West High School, adopted a strict anti-smoking policy for students who faced suspension if they were discovered smoking on campus.

In Oklahoma City and Tulsa public schools, smoking was banned on middle school campuses, but smoking was permitted at designated areas at high school campuses. The teachers' union opposed banning smoking for teachers.

The state legislature added a nickel per pack to the cigarette tax, effective July 1, 1979. The hike pushed vending machine prices to 75 cents per pack. One observer said cigarettes would likely top $1 per pack before gasoline approached $1 per gallon. However, the new tax did not result in any significant reduction in smoking.

CHAPTER SIX

OKLAHOMA STEPS UP ITS GAME

Tobacco-free schools will show our children that we are seriously concerned that their futures be as free as possible of tobacco-related cancer and drug abuse.

— OKLAHOMA GOVERNOR HENRY BELLMON, 1987

Oklahomans who wanted to stop smoking had new resources available in the 1980s. Hundreds of people from across the state descended upon Oklahoma City to attend group hypnosis sessions. For $35, a smoker was allowed to participate in the Damon and Grace Program featuring hypnotist Damon Reinhold. He is credited with using hypnosis to help hundreds of thousands of Americans and Canadians lose weight and stop smoking in group therapy sessions. This method of cessation may have been popular, but has limited evidence of effectiveness.

In 1981, several hundred people jammed into a hotel ballroom in Oklahoma City to try group hypnosis with famed hypnotist Damon Reinhold. In eight sessions, 2,500 Oklahomans attended the sessions. *Courtesy Oklahoma Historical Society.*

The American Lung Association introduced a new 20-day smoking cessation program in 1981. Dr. Everett Rhoades, chief of infectious disease at the University of Oklahoma Health Sciences Center, said the program was based upon years of research and testing. "I wish there was a simple injection we could give a smoker to help him or her stop the habit, but there's not," Dr. Rhoades said. Instead, he heartily endorsed the new program.

In 1982, the U.S. Equal Employment Opportunity Commission, ruled it was not illegal to discriminate against smokers if that was the only basis for discrimination. The National Center for Health Statistics showed that sick smokers cost American businesses $25.8 billion in 1980. The Oklahoma Chapter of the American Cancer Society approved of the federal action and insisted that a man who smoked a pack of cigarettes a day could take 20 breaks in a single shift, thus lowering his productivity.

The American Lung Association's seven-foot "Mr. Cold Turkey" greets people outside the city council meeting in Oklahoma City in 1982. It was time for the annual Cold Turkey Day when smokers across the nation were asked to stop smoking for one day to hopefully begin the journey to cessation. *Courtesy Oklahoma Historical Society.*

Dr. Ed L. Calhoon, a respected physician in Beaver, Oklahoma, authored a resolution at the 1984 meeting of the House of Delegates of the Oklahoma State Medical Association. The resolution asked all physicians to schedule extra time to "explain the extreme hazards of smoking to their patients who smoke." Dr. Calhoon said, "Smoking is a terrible thing—doctors can be influential to get people to quit smoking." Calhoon was one of 12 physicians appointed by President Ronald Reagan to the National Cancer Advisory Board.

Nicotine chewing gum became available by prescription in 1984. Sold under the trade name of Nicorette, the gum was the first anti-smoking substance to have completed extensive clinical and safety tests required by the FDA.

Tobacco industry lobbyists successfully killed a public smoking bill in the 1984 Oklahoma legislative session, prompting the Tobacco Institute to call the victory the "major legislative win" in this region of the country.

As advances were being made in tobacco cessation, the Oklahoma legislature passed a new law effective November 1, 1985, making it a misdemeanor crime to give any tobacco product to a minor. The law was met with skepticism on the editorial page of *The Daily Oklahoman*:

> It is clear the new state law will not stop tobacco use by minors. Machines will continue to supply cigarettes. A black market will develop in smokeless tobacco. Children will smoke and chew tobacco as they always have. Students will return to smoking behind the gymnasium, in the parking lot, and around the school shrubbery.

Instead, the newspaper suggested school officials return to a designated smoking room with large posters on the walls, "pictures of lung cancer . . . yellow teeth and bad breath . . . clothes burned by cinders and stained by tobacco juice."

Fortunately, local school boards began cracking down on student smoking. Many schools prohibited student smoking on school grounds and at school activities. The desire by some superintendents to completely ban smoking was tempered by pressure from residents who insisted that teachers be allowed to smoke in faculty lounges and in outdoor stadiums.

In 1986, Edmond was one of the first Oklahoma cities to ban smoking in public places. The final approved version of the bill applied to half the space of any restaurant, in grocery stores, and hospitals. Mayor Carl Reherman pushed for a stronger law but was opposed by the Oklahoma Restaurant Association. Vince Orza, owner of Garfield's Restaurant and Pub, said, "It's a noble idea—but it's not workable."

Robert L. Tayar, president of Molly Murphy's House of Fine Repute in Oklahoma City and Tulsa, called efforts such as the City of Edmond's "utterly ridiculous." Tayar suggested that the legislature either eliminate smoking entirely in food establishments or let each restaurant decide how much of its space would be set aside for smokers.

Students light a cigarette for "Smoking Sam," a smoking machine used to teach junior high school students the hazards of cigarette smoking.

Courtesy Oklahoma Historical Society.

In 1985, Oklahoma State University became the first public college or university in the state to enact unprecedented restrictions for smokers, chewers, and dippers. The OSU policy prohibited tobacco use in all academic buildings. Smoking in conference rooms was permitted only if approved by a majority vote of the assembled group. "No tobacco" signs were posted throughout academic buildings. Ashtrays were removed from classrooms and hallways.

In the 1980s, 20 years after the Surgeon General's report, the attitude of many Oklahomans was still that tobacco companies should never be held financially liable for smokers' bad health, medical bills, and death. An editorial in *The Daily Oklahoman* the day after Christmas in 1985 echoed the beliefs of many who cheered a California jury's rejection of a wrongful death lawsuit against R.J. Reynolds Tobacco Company:

> Blaming the tobacco firms for cigarette addiction is on the par of irresponsibility with the criminal suspect who pleads innocent because he was too drunk to know what he was doing.
>
> We've become a litigious society. If the lawyer wins his case on appeal, more lawsuits will be filed by people trying to shift the blame for their own indiscretion.

The power and influence of the tobacco industry was on full display in Oklahoma in 1987. The legislature added a provision to Senate Bill 327 to preempt any local law passed to control smoking in public places. The effect was that no city, town, or county could pass a law that was more restrictive than state law. Even if a city wanted to crack down on teenage smoking or smoking in the workplace, it could not because of state laws preempting the field of law.

Tobacco lobbyist and former State Representative Mandell Matheson reported to the Tobacco Institute:

> Ken Nance did one hell of a good job in very difficult circumstances on the smoking law. If you've got to have a law . . . this one is pretty good from our standpoint . . . Ken gave me the task of helping get that [preemption] portion solidified and I was delighted to participate.
>
> I'm hopeful this law will get Oklahoma off the tobacco industry's back for a while.

Oklahoma was only the second state to enact a smoking preemption law. It is still a barrier to stringent local ordinances in 2025, nearly 40 years later.

The Tulsa City Commission felt pressure in 1987 from Oklahoma Tobacco Institute lobbyist Matheson when considering smoking restriction legislation. An internal industry memo later discovered said, "Matheson is working to persuade commissioners that if they enact an ordinance, it should pertain only to city-owned buildings."

Matheson recognized that the possibility of anti-smoking legislation in Oklahoma's second largest city was on the rise. Matheson wrote in a letter to a Tobacco Institute official, "What it actually illustrates, I suppose, is the depth of anti-tobacco feeling here in Tulsa."

The Oklahoma State Department of Health released a study in 1987 that labeled cigarette smoking the most expensive health care problem in the state. Dr. John Harkess, who conducted the department's first survey on the impact of smoking, said cigarette smoking killed 4,700 Oklahomans in 1985 and inflicted more than $600 million in economic losses, including lost earnings and productivity of people who had died prematurely due to smoking.

Oklahoma Governor Henry Bellmon valiantly tried to push a bill through the 1989 legislature that would ban all smoking in Oklahoma public schools. Bellmon said, "Tobacco-free schools will show our children that we are seriously concerned that their futures be as free as possible of tobacco-related cancer and drug abuse."

However, Senator Frank Shurden of Henryetta crippled the bill with an amendment which would allow adults to smoke in designated areas in schools. Ultimately, the legislature passed a bill that left it up to local school boards to regulate smoking in school buildings and on school property.

NOT ENOUGH PROGRESS

Tragically, with the multitude of efforts to convince Americans to quit smoking, the number of cigarette smokers decreased only nine percentage points, from 41% in 1944 to 32% in 1988. The number of female smokers decreased by only six percentage points in the 44 years between the polls. In 1988, 66% of smokers said they would like to give up smoking.

The National Cancer Advisory Board set a goal for the United States to be a tobacco-free society by the year 2000. Little did the panel know how much fight the tobacco companies still had in them.

CHAPTER SEVEN

OKLAHOMA TAKES A STAND

No piece of total smoking restriction legislation has ever been voted on by either house of the Oklahoma State Legislature.

FROM AN R.J. REYNOLDS TOBACCO COMPANY INTERNAL MEMO, 1992

The battles against Big Tobacco helped build the state infrastructure for a strong group of advocates poised and ready to move tobacco control and prevention forward and organized to create impact in the 1990s.

The tobacco industry heavily invested in fighting public health initiatives to regulate tobacco in Oklahoma. Watered-down and ineffective bills had been passed in the 1980s, but efforts to enact smoking regulations in public buildings and in the workplace were slow and unsuccessful.

Courtesy Tulsa World.

In 1992, the Oklahoma House of Representatives passed a bill 79-19 to ban smoking in public schools when students were present. The bill by Republican Representative Carolyn Coleman of Moore would allow adults to smoke outside at events such as baseball, football, and track competitions. The State Senate killed the bill.

Olympic gold medalist Shannon Miller of Edmond, left, with Kay Kloberdanz, center, and Cathy Kerr promoting the programs of the Oklahoma Chapter of the American Lung Association in 1992. Miller told a news conference, "Young people, the kids of Oklahoma, stay away from tobacco. It doesn't make you glamorous and it closes doors to your future." *Courtesy Oklahoma Historical Society.*

Limited progress did come in 1992 when State Representative Mary Fallin of Oklahoma City authored a concurrent resolution asking the Oklahoma Department of Human Services (DHS) to adopt rules banning smoking on the premises of any family day-care home or daycare center. The full House unanimously passed the resolution and the State Senate followed.

In the early 1990s, the Oklahoma State Department of Health (OSDH) took the lead in organizing tobacco control and prevention efforts. A major ally was the Oklahoma Alliance on Health or Tobacco, originally known as the Tobacco Free Oklahoma Coalition (TFOC). The group was made up of the Oklahoma affiliates of the American Cancer Society, American Lung Association, American Heart Association, the Oklahoma State Medical Association, and OSDH.

Successful efforts to suppress anti-smoking legislation were supported by organizations such as the Oklahoma Restaurant Association, the Oklahoma Grocers Association, and the Oklahoma Association of Tobacco & Candy Distributors. The tobacco industry had nurtured strong relationships with these organizations for the purpose of using them as allies and front groups opposing tobacco control legislation.

TFOC released a damning report against cigarette smoking in November 1992. The data showed that smoking-related illnesses cost Oklahomans about $1 billion a year, and cigarette smoking was the leading cause of preventable death and disease in the state. Mike Sulzycki, chairman of TFOC and associate director of the Oklahoma State Medical Association, said tobacco-related diseases killed more Oklahomans than AIDS, accidents, pneumonia, suicide, and diabetes combined.

The 1992 report showed that Oklahoma ranked sixth nationally in the number of women who smoked, and first in the country among women in the 35-64 age group. In addition, more than 6,200 deaths in Oklahoma in 1989 were due to cigarette smoking. A spokeswoman for the Tobacco Institute in Washington, D.C., quarreled with the Oklahoma report. She said each person was well informed about the risks of smoking and had the right and capability to decide for themselves on an individual basis whether or not to use a tobacco product.

When legislators failed to pass statewide bans on smoking in public places, heads of institutions exercised their authority to assist the anti-smoking effort. In 1993, University of Oklahoma President Richard Van Horn instituted the toughest anti-smoking policy in higher education institutions, including banning outdoor smoking at Oklahoma Memorial Stadium during football games. Van Horn said the action underscored the seriousness of OU to ban smoking completely on the Norman campus.

State Representative Ray Vaughn of Edmond began introducing anti-tobacco legislation in the Oklahoma legislature in the early 1990s. *Courtesy Oklahoma Historical Society.*

In 1994, the legislature passed House Bill 2129 to amend the weak 1987 Smoking in Public Places and Indoor Workplaces Act. Finally, restaurants in the state were allowed to voluntarily establish entirely smoke-free facilities. The 1987 law required them to have a smoking section. The 1994 legislature also passed a bill by Representative Ray Vaughn that allowed private businesses to prohibit smoking.

Also in 1994, Congress for the first time, appropriated funds for each state to develop a tobacco use prevention program. Before then, Oklahoma did not have sufficient funds to launch any major effort to reduce tobacco use. Tobacco use prevention and reduction was not a funded priority in OSDH.

With a grant from the Centers for Disease Control and Prevention (CDC), the Office of Tobacco Use Prevention (OTUP) was established in OSDH. Neil Hann was the project director. Doug Matheny, an employee of the OSDH since 1982, was hired as the project coordinator and became director of the Oklahoma IMPACT Project two years later. Matheny credited Hann and Leslie Bennett Webb for crafting a winning grant proposal to secure federal funding for the IMPACT Project.

Doug Matheny earned a master's degree in public health from the University of Oklahoma and saw his work on Oklahoma IMPACT as "an opportunity to have an impact on the health of Oklahomans."

At the federal level, Oklahoma Congressman Mike Synar continued to be involved in anti-smoking efforts. He authored an amendment that required existing federal grants to state substance abuse prevention agencies, including the Oklahoma Department of Mental Health and Substance Abuse Services, be subject to significant reductions if specified standards were not met in compliance with state laws prohibiting sales of tobacco products to minors.

Per CDC's guidance, the Oklahoma IMPACT grant was a collaborative effort to improve state laws around tobacco. OTUP was dedicated to preventing tobacco-related death and disease through a comprehensive effort that included public education, coalition development, and diverse community partnerships.

"The battle was tough," Matheny remembered. "Big Tobacco was well-funded and fought every advance by public health forces in the state."

Matheny said:

> They flouted their strength in front of us. They had fun showing how easily they could defeat any effort we put forth. It was child's play to them.

Matheny felt momentum slowly build from 1994 forward, "The need to reduce tobacco consumption was gradually becoming a clearly defined issue that many legislators and members of the general public could embrace."

Part of OSDH's goal of a state tobacco control plan was to evaluate the effectiveness of tobacco prevention and control activities. The University of Oklahoma College of Public Health was contracted to analyze data and determine trends.

As Oklahoma's efforts to educate the public on the harms of tobacco use were developing, state Attorney General Drew

SMOKING IN THEIR OWN HOUSE

The fight over smoking regulations was not an abstraction for Oklahoma legislators as cigarette smoking was found throughout the State Capitol, including in the House and Senate chambers. It had been a battle, but smoking was finally banned in the legislative chambers in 1993. Even after the turn of the new century, smoking was still allowed in legislators' offices and in the basement smoking room.

Edmondson joined attorneys general from a dozen other states in asking national fast food chains to ban smoking. Arby's was the first chain to ban smoking in corporate-owned restaurants. Dairy Queen and McDonald's soon followed.

In 1995, Representative Vaughn was back with House Bill 1007 to allow local governments to ban smoking in public buildings. State Senator Angela Monson of Oklahoma City co-authored the bill. This bipartisan effort was strongly supported by the Oklahoma Tobacco-Free Coalition. The Oklahoma Municipal League also was in favor of local governments being able to control tobacco.

The bill passed the House of Representatives 64-36. However, vigorous opposition by tobacco lobbyists resulted in the legislation being assigned to a Senate committee which never heard the bill. Tobacco lobbyist Ken Nance told the General Government Committee that current law was adequate because it allowed cities to do everything except ban smoking. The committee voted 9-6 against the bill. The clout of Big Tobacco was real.

After he served in the Oklahoma House of Representatives, Ken Nance became the leader of the lobbying effort of the tobacco companies in the Oklahoma legislature. He was an effective voice for Big Tobacco.

Courtesy Oklahoma Historical Society.

In 1996, Representative Vaughn attempted to repeal the Oklahoma preemption law that Doug Matheny at OSDH said was the "biggest barrier" to reducing tobacco use in the state by prohibiting Oklahoma cities and towns from requiring smoke-free environments inside all public places. Most states had no preemption of local tobacco-related ordinances, allowing their communities to take critical action to protect their citizens against the harms of tobacco.

CHAPTER EIGHT

OKLAHOMA SUES BIG TOBACCO

When we filed our lawsuit, no tobacco company had ever lost in 800 cases, and they had never paid a penny. They believed they were invincible.

— ATTORNEY GENERAL DREW EDMONDSON

The tobacco companies prevailed in every early lawsuit alleging negligence in manufacturing and fraudulent advertising. However, despite the losses, lawsuits prior to the mid-1990s had one positive result; damning secret tobacco company documents were revealed through discovery. The internal memos and research findings were key in convincing later juries that the companies had hidden information that nicotine was addictive and exposed a pattern of fraudulent advertising. Thousands of tobacco company documents were now in the public arena.

In 1992, the U.S. Supreme Court said cigarette makers could be sued under state laws for allegedly deceiving the public about the dangers of smoking. By a 7-2 vote, the high court said federal laws requiring warning labels on cigarette packages did not shield the companies from lawsuits based upon states' personal injury and wrongful death statutes.

In May 1994, the State of Mississippi was the first state to file a lawsuit against the tobacco companies for reimbursement of the state's share of Medicaid expenditures related to treatment of smoking-related illnesses. Mississippi Attorney General Mike Moore became an ally and close friend of Oklahoma Attorney General Edmondson.

Mississippi Attorney General Mike Moore got the ball rolling against Big Tobacco by filing the first lawsuit to recover costs of treating tobacco-related diseases. *Courtesy Mike Moore.*

As the Mississippi case progressed, Moore traveled extensively to encourage the attorneys general in other states to sue the tobacco companies. "I was fired up," Moore said, "I found that the tobacco companies were the most corrupt and evil corporate animal that was ever created in this country. They make a drug, sell it knowing that it's addictive, and then they lie about it."

With the help of tobacco industry whistleblowers Jeffrey Wigand and Merrill Williams, who leaked information that showed the tobacco industry knowingly engineered cigarettes to be addictive, lied about the science, and marketed to youth, the cases against Big Tobacco became viable. The cases were called "righteous lawsuits."

Within months, other states began filing lawsuits. West Virginia was followed by Florida and Minnesota. The cases began revealing additional highly-sensitive tobacco company documents.

> *Nicotine is addictive. We are, then, in the business of selling nicotine, an addictive drug.*
>
> 1963 INTERNAL MEMO FROM GENERAL COUNSEL FOR BROWN & WILLIAMSON

Moore believed that the tobacco industry's deception about the addictive nature of nicotine led to their downfall. "They lied about their products, and they marketed them to kids. But for those two things, they may never have had an Achilles' heel," he said.

In the fall of 1995 and early 1996, Attorney General Edmondson began seeking information about the toll that cigarette smoking was taking on Oklahoma from Matheny at OSDH and others. Edmondson was building a case to be able to file a lawsuit on behalf of the State of Oklahoma against Big Tobacco. He received an unexpected push from the nation's capital.

In May 1996, the U.S. Supreme Court, in the State of Minnesota's case, ordered the tobacco industry defendants to turn over their documents. Tobacco company leaders said there were no "smoking guns" in the databases, but they were wrong.

In August 1996, there was a race to the courthouse by the attorneys general of Oklahoma, Kansas, Arizona, and Michigan. On August 20, 1996, cases were filed in Kansas and Arizona. On August 21, a case was filed in Michigan. Then, on August 22, 1996, Oklahoma became the 14th state to sue the tobacco industry.

What lay ahead for Oklahoma was a major role in the largest and most complex litigation in the history of the United States. Oklahoma's lawsuit was filed in Norman in Cleveland County and asked for $1 billion from 22 defendants.

To announce the lawsuit, Edmondson held a news conference at University Hospital in Oklahoma City and was surrounded by doctors, children from Children's Hospital, and students from the Oklahoma School of Science and Mathematics. He wanted to emphasize the tragedy of young Oklahomans being preyed upon by the tobacco companies. The setting for the announcement of the lawsuit had been suggested by Dr. Robert McCaffree, chief of staff of the Oklahoma City Veterans Administration Hospital and a professor of medicine in the pulmonary disease section of the OU Health Sciences Center.

Oklahoma's lawsuit was unique in one respect. For the first time, the tobacco companies' law firms were named as defendants. The legal theory was that lawyers for the tobacco industry had played a substantive role in deceiving the American public. At the news conference, Edmondson said:

> This lawsuit is based upon the actions of the tobacco industry in the name of profit to mislead and misguide the American people on a matter of public health over the last four decades. They have manipulated nicotine levels to increase the addictive qualities of cigarettes, and they have engaged in a multibillion-dollar advertising campaign aimed at children.

Edmondson said Oklahoma taxpayers had paid more than $900 million from 1980 to 1993 as the state's portion of Medicaid to pay for treatment for tobacco-related illnesses. Edmondson called out the heads of tobacco companies for allowing cartoon characters such as Joe Camel to be nearly as popular with children as Mickey Mouse. "We want them to come clean," Edmondson said.

Edmondson knew Big Tobacco would come out swinging. "Make no mistake about it," he said. "This lawsuit is going to be a knock-down, drag-out affair. These folks play hardball."

The attorney general's office did not have sufficient staff to prosecute the case so contingent fee contracts were signed with three highly respected Oklahoma law firms. John Norman had won major jury verdicts over a quarter century after graduating from the OU College of Law in 1968. He was the senior partner at Norman, Edem, McNaughton & Wallace in Oklahoma City. Also from the firm was Tom Wallace, a Columbia University law graduate, president of the Oklahoma Trial Lawyers Association.

The other law firms were Riggs, Abney, Neal, Turpen, Orbison & Lewis, led by former State Representative and trial lawyer, David Riggs, former Oklahoma Attorney General Mike Turpen, and Robert "Bob" Nance, a former Oklahoma assistant attorney general. Pray, Walker, Jackman, Williamson & Marlar, with offices in Oklahoma City and Tulsa, was the third law firm.

Serving as Chief Liaison Attorney for the state was Henry "Hank" Meyer, III, a former legislative assistant to Oklahoma Congressman James R. Jones and chair of the board of the Indigent Defense System of Oklahoma. Key contacts in the attorney general's office were First Assistant Attorney General Neal Leader and Assistant Attorneys General David Hudson and Tom Gruber.

Edmondson hired Norman attorney Preston A. Trimble as local counsel for the lawsuit. Trimble knew the courthouse in Norman "like the back of his hand." For 29 years, he was either elected as district attorney or district judge in Cleveland County.

Edmondson's prediction that the Oklahoma lawsuit would not be easy was proved in the months after the lawsuit was filed. Millions of documents were reviewed. The Oklahoma trial team consisted of 89 lawyers, 83 paralegals, and 72 clerks. The enormity of the Oklahoma case against Big Tobacco is hard to believe:

- 168 defense lawyers entered an appearance
- 578 defense requests for production of documents
- 206 defense interrogatories
- 103 million Medicaid records
- 25 state agencies involved
- 531,000 plaintiff documents produced
- 40 trial court hearings
- 200 depositions
- 349 witnesses listed by Oklahoma; 168 by defendants

The tobacco companies produced hundreds of cardboard boxes of documents. Lawyers and staff carefully plowed through the documents and occasionally found a gem. In files from the Tobacco Institute, a 1979 letter was found from the Oklahoma Association of Tobacco Distributors that bragged that a bill to limit tobacco smoking was dead and would not come out of a Senate committee. The letter said, "The Chairman is well known to one of our stronger tobacco distributors and we have elicited the

Chairman's promise that the resolution will remain in committee for the balance of the year."

A 1989 Philip Morris memo said:

> In Oklahoma, the industry lobby team is absolutely superb and seems to be able to hold leadership in coming out in the press against a cigarette tax every time the Governor brings it up, which is often. All the lobbyists were former members and just do a great job.

Oklahoma was required to produce hundreds of thousands of pages of documents. At the OSDH, Doug Matheny and his staff converted a former lunch break room to house a dozen copy machines. Matheny remembered, "Tobacco industry workers, with lawyers leading the effort, went through huge stacks of boxes of paper. It was a constant job from early morning to late at night."

Cleveland County District Judge Tom Lucas set aside one day a month to hear motions in the case that had become one of the largest and most unwieldy of the states' lawsuits. Defense attorneys for the tobacco industry told Judge Lucas the Oklahoma case was different from the cases filed in the other states and was more complex to defend.

Bitter verbal battles took place in Judge Lucas' courtroom. Edmondson wanted to take the deposition of former Oklahoma State Senator Ken Nance who was a registered lobbyist for the Tobacco Institute. Edmondson wanted Nance to tell how much money had been spent by Big Tobacco to influence votes of the state legislature.

Bob Nance, a lawyer for the Oklahoma legal team and no kin to tobacco lobbyist Ken Nance, said preparation was intense because it was anticipated that the tobacco companies would force Oklahoma to trial. "Big Tobacco was a formidable opponent," Nance said. "The tobacco industry hired the best defense and corporate lawyers in the country to try to wear us down." Bob Nance remembered, "They were confident because they had never lost, until the truth began coming out about their knowledge that nicotine was addictive and that advertising was directed toward children."

In early 1997, there were secret talks among lawyers for the states and tobacco companies. In July 1997, the lawsuit in Mississippi was settled on the eve of trial. The following month, the same happened in Florida. In January 1998, Texas settled just before the trial began. In May, Minnesota's case was settled while the jury was deliberating.

Meanwhile, after tens of thousands of hours spent by the legal team, the Oklahoma case was the next in line to be set for jury trial to begin in January 1999.

Settlement talks by dozens of states were ramping up. Attorney General Edmondson said Oklahoma was willing to get on board and endorsed a plan for the states to broker a settlement with Big Tobacco. Edmondson was one of nine state attorneys general selected to negotiate a master settlement with the tobacco companies.

The tobacco industry is the only truly evil legal industry in the United States. I define evil as somebody who knowingly and willingly harms others for their own enrichment.

— DR. ROBERT MCCAFFREE

CHAPTER NINE

THE SETTLEMENT

It was the biggest advance in public health since the discovery of the polio vaccine.

— MISSISSIPPI ATTORNEY GENERAL MIKE MOORE

The litigation against Big Tobacco was ripe for settlement. More than 40 states had sued tobacco companies for billions of dollars. The legal theory that cigarettes caused diseases that resulted in significant costs to the states' public health systems was working. Tobacco companies faced bankruptcy if they lost all the cases.

Negotiations between the attorneys general, made up of both Republicans and Democrats, and leaders of the tobacco industry and their lawyers took place in New York City after months of private talks. "It was a tough sell," Edmondson said, "You're asking an industry to fund messages not to buy their product."

Sponsorships were a "big deal" for the tobacco companies. Edmondson remembered, "R.J. Reynolds walked out of the negotiations once when we were squeezing their advertising dollars. They wanted to keep the Winston Cup, the sponsorship of a popular race." The disagreement was so strong, Edmondson thought for a while the states would settle against Philip Morris and Lorillard and go to trial against R.J. Reynolds and Brown & Williamson. In the end, the states agreed that each company could keep one sponsorship, but it could not involve children in any way.

In June 1997, Mike Moore, Edmondson, and the other attorneys general held a news conference. Edmondson remembered, "I never had seen so many microphones and cameras. There was huge public interest worldwide of what might come out of a possible settlement."

The parties sought a congressional remedy first. The settlement included a payment of nearly $400 billion, stronger warning labels, restrictions on advertising, and FDA regulation under certain circumstances. In exchange, the tobacco companies would be free from class-action suits and litigation costs.

The attorneys general did not have authority to make their side of the settlement agreement happen so the Global Settlement Agreement would require an act of Congress. U.S. Senator John McCain of Arizona carried the bill. However, in the spring of 1998, after extensive debate and deliberations, Congress rejected the settlement. Moore said, "Our only alternative was to go back to the negotiating table even though Mississippi, Florida, Texas, and Minnesota worked out individual settlements for their states."

On November 23, 1998, the attorneys general of the remaining 46 states and the District of Columbia, Puerto Rico, and the

Attorney General Drew Edmondson at a news conference in Oklahoma City outlining Oklahoma's share of the Master Settlement Agreement.

Virgin Islands, signed the newly-negotiated Master Settlement Agreement with the four largest cigarette manufacturers, Philip Morris USA, R.J. Reynolds Tobacco Company, Brown & Williamson Tobacco Corp., and Lorillard Tobacco Company. Later, most of the other tobacco companies that produced cigarettes signed the same agreement.

The MSA's purpose was to reduce smoking in the United States, especially among youth. It was to be achieved through:

- Raising the cost of cigarettes by imposing huge payment obligations on the tobacco companies
- Banning the use of cartoons in advertising, packaging, or labeling
- Prohibiting tobacco companies from distributing merchandise bearing the name of tobacco products
- Banning payment to promote tobacco products in movies, television shows, theater, music, and video games
- Prohibiting tobacco brand name sponsorship of events with a significant youth audience or team sports
- Establishing and funding the Truth Initiative, an organization "dedicated to achieving a culture where all youth and young adults reject tobacco"
- Providing money for the states in perpetuity to use to fund smoking prevention programs

In addition, the tobacco companies agreed to disband the Tobacco Institute and other similar groups and to fund the

In 2024, former Oklahoma Attorney General Drew Edmondson reviewed the massive 1998 Master Settlement Agreement between 46 states and the major tobacco companies. *Courtesy Gini Moore Campbell.*

National Public Education Foundation, dedicated to reducing youth smoking and preventing diseases associated with smoking. The tobacco companies also paid the states' legal fees.

The states were to receive an estimated $206 billion the first 25 years of the agreement. It was by far the largest lawsuit settlement in history. There was an up-front payment of $12.7 billion with an estimated $9 billion per year as long as cigarettes are sold in the United States.

The exact amount Oklahoma and each of the other states and territories receive under the MSA was based primarily upon the number of cigarettes sold in 1997 and in future years.

The payment from the tobacco companies was deposited in an escrow account until the states created a mechanism for receiving and spending the money. Many states allowed their legislatures to decide how to spend the money. A quarter century later, only a small percentage of MSA money is used to implement comprehensive, statewide tobacco prevention and control programs. Oklahoma is an exception.

CHAPTER TEN

THE DEBATE OVER HOW TO SPEND THE MONEY

Two billion dollars coming to Oklahoma attracted a lot of attention.

— ATTORNEY GENERAL DREW EDMONDSON

In November 1998, Attorney General Edmondson talked to reporters about Oklahoma's share of the tobacco settlement at a news conference at the National Press Club in Washington, D.C. Edmondson said the Oklahoma portion of the settlement would be more than $2 billion. Edmondson said, "I will sign the settlement agreement with pride and assurance that we continue to work so the children of my state will be safer in the future."

Within a short time, Oklahoma's elected officials and state agency leaders began formulating ideas of how to spend the $2 billion. State Health Commissioner Dr. Jerry Nida was one of the first to propose that the bulk of the state's share of the settlement be spent on tobacco control and prevention programs. He said, "After all, it was tobacco victims who paid the price for the settlement."

Bob Miner, chair of the Tobacco Free Oklahoma Coalition, and Doug Matheny, director of OSDH's Office of Tobacco Use Prevention, echoed Dr. Nida's sentiments. Matheny said he believed that a significant amount of the settlement money should be spent on implementing best practices in tobacco control: prevent young people from starting, promoting cessation, eliminating exposure to secondhand smoke, and identifying and eliminating high rates of smoking and tobacco-related deaths among certain communities.

A few legislators wanted to use the money to build highways, bridges, prisons, and other infrastructure projects. The State Council on Aging suggested part of the money be used to cover long-term care for senior citizens suffering from tobacco-related illnesses. The Department of Human Services proposed using some of the money to fund the state ombudsman's program, which oversees care in nursing homes.

George Humphreys, research director of the Oklahoma House of Representatives, began looking at how other states planned to spend their share of the settlement. Humphreys was aware that Congress was considering mandating expenditures and wanted Oklahoma to "beat Congress to the punch." He talked with State Representative Jari Askins of Duncan about the possibility of establishing a trust so the funds could be invested.

Askins scheduled a series of meetings with interested parties. Participants included representatives of the governor, attorney general, and state treasurer; directors of several state agencies, including the Oklahoma State Department of Health; leaders of the Tobacco Free Oklahoma Coalition; and legislative staff.

Askins and State Senator Ben Brown filed House Bill 1002 which would put the tobacco money in a trust fund, a "statutory trust fund," a creation of the state legislature which could change its terms and conditions later. Askins fielded questions from many legislators who believed the legislature should decide how to spend the money. Askins said, "For a state with a lot of needs, that was very, very tempting."

State Senator Ben Brown was a leading advocate of putting the tobacco settlement money in a trust fund. "There was a huge push to put the money in the general revenue fund," he said. "At the Capitol, there's never enough money to go around. The tobacco money would have been lost in the annual budgeting process." *Courtesy Oklahoma Historical Society.*

House Bill 1002 directed that most of the tobacco funds be spent on tobacco programs, especially to curb minors' access to tobacco products. The bill was passed by large margins in both houses of the legislature but was vetoed by Governor Frank Keating.

Askins did not believe the governor had a hidden motive. She remembered, "I believe he thought it was the legislature that had a hidden motive. He was concerned about legislators' plans for the money."

State Representative and later Lieutenant Governor Jari Askins wanted to prevent the tobacco settlement funds from becoming part of the normal legislative appropriations process. *Courtesy Oklahoma Historical Society.*

Keating later said, "I vetoed the bill because I thought it was premature to set up a trust before any plans were made how to spend the money. It would have been a mistake to turn $2 billion over to the vagaries of the legislative political process."

Keating had a good record of supporting anti-smoking measures. In his first term, he created the Governor's Task Force on Tobacco and Youth. He also publicly opposed the state's preemption of stricter clean air and anti-smoking ordinances in cities and towns.

Askins and Representative Ray Vaughn tried to create a trust fund with another bill during the 1999 session. However, the bill never got out of a House committee because leadership did not have a commitment from the governor that he would sign the measure.

The results of a statewide poll showed 90% of Oklahomans favored spending at least some of the settlement funds to prevent or reduce tobacco use among kids. Of those polled, 61% thought more than half the money should be used for prevention.

Governor Keating said he would like to see a significant contribution made to the Oklahoma Teachers' Retirement System from the settlement money. And the governor proposed issuing bonds to finance a variety of state government projects and using the tobacco annual payments to repay the bonds. The idea was to securitize or take a discount on the projected payout to receive cash.

Keating said he did not believe the revenue stream from the tobacco companies would continue for 25 years and Oklahoma should issue bonds instead of counting on receiving annual payments.

Keating's plan drew immediate criticism. Attorney General Edmondson used his bully pulpit as the attorney general who helped negotiate the tobacco settlement to tell a news conference:

> The overriding principle ought to be that this was a public health issue, it was a public health lawsuit, it is a public health win, and that's where the money ought to be directed. The lion's share of the money should be spent on public health.

State Senator Ben "Bulldog" Robinson, a staunch supporter of anti-smoking legislation, remembered that tobacco lobbyists showed up every week, "taking several people out to dinner to try to convince us to sell big a bond issue and pay for the bonds with annual tobacco payments."

Robinson said the tobacco lobbyists were "stout." They threw dinners and invited legislators to golf tournaments. "Their lobbyists were the best. They had the brightest minds. They knew what to do," he said.

In June 1999, Governor Keating expressed another opinion of how to spend the money. He said his first choice was to finance a $350 million higher education bond issue. The following month, the governor used a news release to say "every penny" of the state's tobacco money should be spent on education, including teachers' pay raises, technology, and infrastructure. Keating said using money for state agencies to fund smoking prevention programs would dilute the effectiveness of the tobacco dollars.

Governor Frank Keating stirred the debate over what to do with the tobacco settlement money. Looking back at 2000, Keating said, "I wanted to promote a robust discussion of all options. In the end, TSET was the correct solution."

Courtesy Oklahoma Historical Society.

Dr. Robert McCaffree, chair of the Tobacco Free Oklahoma Coalition, disagreed with the governor. Dr. McCaffree said, "The education should be about tobacco products and their use first. Otherwise, we are simply sacrificing our children under the rubric of education." McCaffree said programs on

A BONUS FOR OKLAHOMA

In March 1999, Oklahoma received a $267.8 million bonus because of its strategic role in the historic tobacco litigation. A group of former state attorneys general evaluated the contributions of the various states in putting the tobacco companies on their heels and making them amenable to settlement. Lawyers for Oklahoma won several important motions in the state lawsuit in Cleveland County, and those decisions helped other states in their lawsuits.

Attorney General Edmondson said several of his assistants, including Senior Assistant Attorney General Neal Leader, Assistant Attorney General Mitty Mohanty, and paralegal Lori Sheltman spent hundreds of hours helping outside counsel get ready for what the legal team thought would be a jury trial in Norman in 1999.

Dr. Robert McCaffree was a highly respected pulmonologist and a leader of Oklahoma's anti-smoking effort. He was a past president of the American College of Chest Surgeons, the only national group that filed an amicus curiae brief in the Mississippi case against Big Tobacco.
Courtesy Oklahoma Historical Society.

prevention and cessation of smoking were the "foundation stones" of a comprehensive anti-tobacco-use strategy. McCaffree said:

> States that spent the most money on effective comprehensive prevention and cessation programs have experienced the largest declines in tobacco consumption.
>
> If you have a problem, you don't want to keep pouring money into ameliorating it. You want to pour money into preventing the problem in the first place.

Representative Vaughn said he wanted to see funds used for the "purpose they were intended for," to reduce smoking and addiction to nicotine. Vaughn also said a focus of the tobacco settlement money should be on "keeping our children from becoming users of tobacco."

The executive director of the Oklahoma State Medical Association, Brian Foy, had the harshest criticism of the governor's plan. Foy said he was "extremely disappointed" with the governor's proposal. Foy said, "The tobacco settlement monies offer a tremendous opportunity to make a difference in the health of the public and the future health of our children."

The editorial page of *The Daily Oklahoman* had its opinion:

> In no way should this state's share of the tobacco settlement money be spent as part of the normal appropriations process. Instead, it should be invested. It should not be viewed as a quick fix to any particular problem. Instead of consuming the money as fast as it comes in, Oklahoma should create an endowment that will last well into the next century.

The Oklahoma State Regents for Higher Education made its own proposal in August 1999. Chancelor Hans Brisch said higher education should play a vital role in curbing chronic disease. In a strongly-worded resolution, regents said a college education led to less tobacco use. The regents suggested using $500 million of the tobacco money to build a cancer research facility in Oklahoma City with a satellite clinic in Tulsa.

The Daily Oklahoman suggested there would be a big battle over tobacco money in the 2000 legislature. The newspaper editorialized, "The wagons are circling the state legislature more than three months from the start of its session . . . we believe the state's share ought to be spent primarily for health care."

Governor Keating had another idea for use of the money in November 1999. He wanted to use $125 million to shore up rural hospitals. Keating had learned of 25 rural hospitals that were in danger of closing because of the reduction in Medicare reimbursement rates. Critics supported helping rural hospitals, just not with tobacco settlement money.

Attorney General Edmondson's opinion was strengthened by State Treasurer Robert Butkin who became a "champion" of the idea for a trust fund that was not accessible to the legislative appropriations process.

State Treasurer Robert Butkin became an outspoken advocate for placing the tobacco settlement money into a trust fund not part of the legislative appropriations process. *Courtesy Tulsa World.*

House Speaker Loyd Benson and State Senate President Pro Tempore Stratton Taylor endorsed the trust fund idea. Taylor said, "There are many people who are going to be grabbing for these dollars, so let's make certain they really go for what they were intended."

The Governor's Task Force on Tobacco and Youth requested that the state spend $54 million annually on cessation and prevention programs for Oklahoma's youth. Task Force chair, Representative Vaughn, said:

> Without implementation of a comprehensive, effective statewide tobacco use prevention and reduction program, Oklahoma will continue to lose the war against childhood nicotine addiction and tremendous unnecessary human and economic costs will result.

House Speaker Loyd Benson of Frederick was co-author of the bill that sent the TSET constitutional amendment to a vote of the people in 2000.

Courtesy Oklahoma Historical Society.

Mississippi Attorney General Moore came to Oklahoma City in March 2000 to urge the legislature to "spend the money on what the fight was about," noting that setting any higher priority for the money would amount to "moral treason." Moore talked about his home state which had approved a comprehensive pilot program to curb teen-smoking. The remainder of the money was going into a trust. Moore urged Oklahoma to do the same.

Governor Keating and the legislature continued to go in different directions on spending the first $37 million installment of tobacco money. The House wanted to spend the money on a health initiative. The Governor wanted to use some of the money to cut state income taxes.

The Oklahoman and the University of Oklahoma collaborated in a poll in April 2000 to determine how the citizens of the state thought the tobacco money should be spent. Fifty nine percent of those polled believed the legislature should put all settlement money into trust and spend only the interest. More than half were against using the money to reduce taxes.

Gary Copeland, an OU political science professor and adviser for the poll, found the response to the tax cut question interesting. He said:

> I think people see this as an opportunity to do something and not just fritter the money away with a marginal tax cut when in fact we have this opportunity to deal with some real needs in this state.

President Pro Tempore Taylor appointed State Senator Robinson as chair of a special committee to draft legislation to allocate the tobacco settlement money. When Robinson asked Taylor what senators were on the committee, Taylor said, "You pick them." Robinson chose State Senators Angela Monson and Bernest Cain because they agreed with him that a trust fund outside the reach of the legislature would be best.

> *History will judge us harshly if we do not use settlement funds first and foremost to effectively reduce the number of Oklahoma children becoming addicted to deadly tobacco products.*
>
> — STATE REPRESENTATIVE RAY VAUGHN

As the end of the legislative session drew near, Governor Keating continued to promote selling Oklahoma's interest in tobacco settlement money to investors who would pay cash for the state to invest. Keating wanted to use the first payment to buy bonds to build a national weather center in Norman, a cancer center, and bail out rural hospitals.

Keating's position lost steam after a three-member panel, headed by State Treasurer Butkin, suggested the money be placed into a trust. Butkin said, "The soundest employment of the tobacco settlement monies, from both a fiscal and ethical perspective, is the creation of a long-term permanent trust fund."

The votes were there to create a trust fund. Butkin said:

> People were working together across the political spectrum, across the cultural spectrum, and across the economic spectrum. Business and community leaders came together and said, "OK, what makes sense for Oklahoma? Do we want to use this money to build bridges or schools? Or do we want to address the extraordinarily high cost that our society has incurred because of tobacco?"

Behind the scenes, Attorney General Edmondson and President Pro Tempore Taylor negotiated the language of House Bill 2022 that would define the constitutional amendment to be voted on by the people. Edmondson insisted that the constitutional trust eventually receive 75% of the tobacco money.

If the legislature did not agree to that number, an initiative petition drive would be launched to completely bypass the legislature and put 100% of the settlement money into the trust. That possibility convinced Taylor to agree to 75%.

Five days before the end of the session, House Speaker Benson and Senate leader Taylor met with House and Senate conferees to unveil the proposed language of the legislation. House Bill 2022, passed by both houses, proposed a constitutional amendment to be placed on the November 7 general election ballot.

Under the measure, at least 50% of the tobacco settlement money would be put into the "Tobacco Settlement Endowment Trust Fund" (TSET) beginning in fiscal year 2002 with the contribution increased by five percentage points each year until 2007 when the trust fund deposit would be 75%.

State Senate President Pro Tempore Stratton Taylor of Claremore was an architect of the constitutional amendment that created TSET. Taylor said, "The people were wise to secure the bulk of the tobacco money in the trust so that programs to reduce smoking and tobacco use in the state could be funded far into the future."

Courtesy Oklahoma Historical Society.

The House passed the bill 97-2 and the Senate approved the measure 33-8. Senator Brown said, "This will be a legacy for the people of Oklahoma long after this body is gone."

The proposed constitutional amendment would set up a Board of Investors made up of the State Treasurer, who was the chair; an appointee of the governor; an appointee of the House Speaker; an appointee of the Senate Pro Tempore; and an appointee of the State Auditor and Inspector.

In addition, a Board of Directors of TSET would consist of seven members, one each appointed by the Governor, Senate President Pro Tempore, House Speaker, the Attorney General, the State Treasurer, the State Auditor and Inspector, and the State Superintendent of Public Instruction.

The proposed amendment became State Question 692. The amendment mandated that earnings from the trust fund be spent on:

- Research for the purpose of enhancing efforts to prevent and combat cancer and other tobacco-related diseases
- Cost-effective tobacco prevention and cessation programs
- Other programs to maintain or improve the health of Oklahomans, with emphasis on children
- School programs and substance abuse programs to improve the quality of life and health of children
- Programs to enhance the health and well-being of senior adults.

Attorney General Edmondson and State Treasurer Butkin were co-chairmen of the Oklahoma Coalition on Health and Tobacco, formed to promote passage of State Question 692. The coalition included Governor Keating, First Lady Cathy Keating, Lieutenant Governor Mary Fallin, and legislative leaders.

Interested groups and individuals contributed about $250,000 for advertising expenses. *The Oklahoman* and the *Tulsa World* asked state voters to approve the trust. So did dozens of newspapers in cities and towns. Many applauded the efforts of Edmondson and Butkin for wanting the tobacco dollars in a trust fund earmarked for better health care, particularly to address health difficulties linked to tobacco use.

It was truly a bipartisan effort. Republicans, Governor Keating, Lieutenant Governor Mary Fallin, and Labor Commissioner Brenda Reneau Wynn, joined Edmondson, Butkin, and other Democratic leaders in backing the proposal.

On election day, Oklahoma voters overwhelmingly approved State Question 692 by more than 424,000 votes, 68.8 to 31.2%.

TSET was a reality. The proceeds of the tobacco settlement money were protected for future generations.

Buttons used in 2000 to garner support for the state question to create TSET.

CHAPTER ELEVEN

A FIRM FOOTING

Oklahoma was the only state to create a constitutional trust to protect its share of the 1998 tobacco settlement, a decision that has been hailed by leaders and experts in Oklahoma and across the nation.

State Treasurer Butkin convened the first TSET Board of Investors in a conference room on the first floor of the State Capitol on May 22, 2001. It was the job of the Board of Investors to develop an investment policy to grow the funds received each year as safely and quickly as possible. Butkin was pleased that statutes and the constitutional amendment authorized the Board of Investors to hire, through a competitive bidding process and evaluation, trained and expert professional money managers.

On August 16, 2001, the TSET Board of Directors met for the first time at the Oklahoma Historical Society, now the Oklahoma Judicial Center, southeast of the State Capitol. Dr. Robert McCaffree, Attorney General Edmondson's appointment to the board, was selected as the first chairman of the group. Other original board members were:

- Dr. Donald Cooper of Stillwater was called the "father of sports medicine." He was the team doctor for the 1968 U.S. Olympic team and member of the President's Council on Sports, Fitness & Nutrition.
- Dr. Suzanne Olive was a pulmonary and allergy physician in Tulsa who had cared for many patients with disorders related to tobacco use.
- Brian Maddy had been chief of staff for State Senate Pro Tempore Stratton Taylor. He was familiar with the TSET enabling legislation.
- Tracy Foor was an award-winning high school teacher from Norman.
- Marvin Apple was a longtime health administrator from Tahlequah. He was committed to community-based programs.
- Oklahoma City attorney and CPA Susan Walters Bize who had been president of the Oklahoma Chapter of the American Cancer Society and promoted public health activities.

Dr. McCaffree opened the first TSET Board of Directors meeting with his idea about the focus of the group:

> These monies belong to the people of Oklahoma. These monies are here because of the evils the tobacco companies have perpetrated on the citizens of our state. Because of the tremendous heartache and spending on tobacco-related

illnesses, the tobacco companies owe Oklahoma because they have cost the citizens greatly.

TSET had two boards, but no staff. Nancy Anthony, former executive director of the Oklahoma City Community Foundation, coordinated meetings and invited the boards to meet at the Foundation offices. The Board of Directors wanted input from many stakeholders, so public forums were scheduled for government agencies and anti-smoking groups to submit ideas and proposals for TSET moving forward. Dr. McCaffree said, "The forums gave us ideas of what people would like to see and helped direct our thoughts."

There were many ideas from citizens and government agency personnel. Dr. McCaffree remembered, "There also were ideas that were bad, but amusing." One suggestion was that TSET develop fishing areas around the state so parents could take their children fishing. They reasoned that if the children were fishing, they were less likely to smoke.

The state health department released a report from the CDC in October 2001 that showed Oklahoma's baseline for tobacco use—a starting point for TSET's work to reduce the toll of tobacco:

- 23% of adult Oklahomans smoked; 30% of teenagers smoked or used tobacco products.
- Oklahoma had the ninth-highest smoking-related death rate in the U.S.
- Each year 6,000 Oklahomans died prematurely from smoking-related diseases.
- Exposure to secondhand smoke caused an estimated 750 deaths a year.
- Illnesses and lost productivity related to tobacco cost $1 billion a year.
- More than 14,000 Oklahoma teenagers began using tobacco products each year.

The original $50 million TSET fund earned $651,619 the first year, prompting *The Oklahoman* to editorialize, "The state tobacco settlement trust fund has started doing what it was created to do—earn interest." The Board of Directors approved money for the TSET Board of Investors to hire investment advisers and fund managers and choose a custodial bank to handle TSET's assets. The Board of Directors had until January 1, 2002, to devise a master plan for the use of the earnings.

TSET's first employee was Tracey Strader who was named executive director in 2002. Strader, who held a Masters of Social Work Administration degree from OU, had spent many years working in the behavioral health system with groups that smoked at higher rates and suffered the consequences. Strader also worked in the Tobacco Use Prevention Service for several years after developing the state health department's first programs to help expectant mothers stop smoking. She remembered:

Oklahoma Tobacco Settlement Endowment Trust

> From the start, I was motivated to get the message out that smoking was not just an adult choice like the tobacco companies said. The companies were deliberately preying on our youth and causing so much death and disease, all for a profit.

Strader knew about the creation of TSET and was "thrilled that the money would be earmarked for the purposes that it was intended." She had attended TSET board meetings the first year and understood the board's goals.

As a foundation for future grants, the TSET Board of Directors looked to the Oklahoma State Plan for Tobacco Use Prevention and Cessation, created by the OSDH. The board funded grants to begin to implement key components of a comprehensive tobacco control program.

Strader was executive director for nearly 14 years until 2017, more than half the life of TSET to date. Looking back, she said, "It was genius in the way the board was set up, from different geographical areas and appointed by different elected officials. It takes politics out of the equation."

TSET's efforts worked in conjunction with a coalition of three state agencies that declared war on tobacco. New Department of Health Commissioner Leslie Beitsch emerged as a formidable foe and leader of the coalition.

Beitsch, of Florida, was tapped by the State Board of Health to raise the alarm on tobacco use in Oklahoma. During his brief tenure, with the backing of the Board of Health, great strides were made in reducing exposure to secondhand smoke.

An early TSET staff, from left, Sjonna Paulson, Jonás Mata, Tracey Strader, Sharon Neal, Dorothy Antwine, and Carol Hernandez.

"I felt like I was given the mission and the permission to do what I needed to do," Beitsch said. "That just felt like great alignment."

Beitsch was a change agent and began using rulemaking powers to reduce exposure to secondhand smoke. In January 2002, smoking was banned in health departments, then healthcare facilities, and most public places. Governor Keating followed by signing rules that required restaurants with more than 50 seats to be completely smoke-free. Health inspections by OSDH would confirm if restaurants were complying.

"When we could not get all the votes we needed in the legislature, we began a strategy of rulemaking. We were constantly ratcheting up the rulemaking process to be more and more comprehensive to cover as many things as we could," Bietsch said. "All of that was to keep the issue very much front and center when the legislature wanted to keep it off the radar."

Beitsch also unveiled a plan that asked the legislature for $31 million in annual funding, a cigarette tax of $1 per pack, stronger restrictions on youth access to tobacco products, repealing preemption of local tobacco ordinances, and new statewide laws that would promote smoke-free public places.

Terry Cline, commissioner of the Department of Mental Health and Substance Abuse Services, and Mike Fogarty, CEO of the Oklahoma Health Care Authority, helped develop the strategy in breakfast meetings with Beitsch. It was not long before they realized tobacco was their biggest concern and top priority.

The coalition counted on broad public support. Beitsch said, "Seventy-seven percent of the people in Oklahoma don't smoke, and I think they are tired of breathing other people's smoke."

In April 2002, the CDC released a report on teenage tobacco use. Oklahoma high school students were the sixth heaviest users in the nation at 42% behind West Virginia, Kentucky, Montana, Wyoming, and Arkansas. The report also showed that 21% of middle school students in Oklahoma smoked cigarettes or used other tobacco products.

Also in 2002, State Treasurer Butkin proposed another constitutional amendment that would change how much of the TSET money could be spent by the Board of Directors each year. The original amendment in 2000 allowed only the earnings of the trust fund to be spent. The legislature quickly passed the call for Oklahomans to vote on the change which would allow the TSET board to spend up to 5.5% of the value of the trust fund each year. Butkin's reasoning was that during economic downturns, the fund would not have any earnings and ongoing programs would suffer.

Even though there appeared to be no organized opposition to State Question 701 on the November 5, 2002, general election ballot, voters did not like the idea. They were resolute in protecting the trust fund's future. The state question was defeated 55% to 45%.

The 2003 legislature took care of the fact that "earnings" were not defined in the constitutional amendment that created TSET. House Bill 1457, sponsored by House Speaker Larry Adair and Representative Askins, defined earnings as dividends and interest cash from investments. Before the change, the directors were limited to spending only the amount that the trust fund had appreciated in value.

Also in 2003, the legislature passed the Smoking in Public Places and Indoor Workplaces Act, which required most indoor public places to be smoke-free. However, the strong tobacco lobby was able to assure that the law retained preemptive language, exempting all free-standing bars, allowed restaurants to serve customers in smoking rooms, and allowed all workplaces to provide smoking rooms in which no work could be performed.

In April 2003, TSET announced the creation of its first major program, telephone counseling for smokers through the Oklahoma Tobacco Helpline. As the TSET trust fund topped $100 million in 2003, earnings allowed TSET to begin addressing Oklahoma's leading cause of preventable death on a statewide basis. The U.S. Public Health Service had concluded that telephone counseling was one of the most effective smoking cessation strategies. The Helpline had the ability to serve tens of thousands of Oklahomans with an effective intervention statewide. That powerful reach helped drive down the state's smoking rates. In-person cessation programs did not compare to the Helpline's ability to reach Oklahoma tobacco users in all corners of the state 24-hours a day, 7-days a week.

On August 20, 2003, Governor Brad Henry, State Treasurer Butkin, Attorney General Edmondson, and Dr. McCaffree appeared at a State Capitol news conference to formally kick off the Oklahoma Tobacco Helpline. The telephone number was 866-PITCH EM or 866-748-2436, initially conceived in 2001 as part of a local tobacco control "demonstration project" in Tulsa funded with limited state monies allocated by the legislature to the state health department. The helpline was operated by a nonprofit company, Group Health Cooperative. The cost for the first year of operation was $475,000, funded entirely by earnings from TSET's trust fund.

Professional counselors, called "quit coaches," staffed the helpline and worked with participants to create and move them through a personalized quit-smoking plan. Evaluation results have consistently shown a high rate of success and positive participant experience.

In 2004, Oklahoma was in danger of losing federal money because of weak state laws prohibiting the sale of tobacco products to minors. Senate Bill 1256, authored by State Senator "Bulldog" Robinson, was approved by the legislature and signed into law by Governor Henry. The law prohibited self-service tobacco displays. It also required stores to place tobacco products behind the counter, requiring customers to ask a clerk for assistance, making it easier to check the age of the buyer. The new law also held the owner of the store liable if a clerk was caught selling to minors three times. Senator Robinson said, "If we can stop our children from starting to smoke, we can save lives. It really is just that simple."

The 2004 legislature also voted to submit to the people a 55-cent-per-pack cigarette tax hike. Senate President Pro Tempore Cal Hobson said the measure was the most important issue passed by the legislature since a school reform measure in 1990.

Attorney General Edmondson was out front in support of the ballot measure. Commenting on tobacco-company sponsored television ads opposing the proposal, Edmondson said:

> Why in the world would we believe them? They have been lying to us for half a century. There is no reason that Oklahoma should be in the bottom five of the states in terms of tobacco tax.

Dr. McCaffree also bashed the tobacco company ads. He said, "Have they no shame?" McCaffree supported the tax hike as one of the most effective ways to reduce childhood smoking was to increase the price of cigarettes. "It makes it more expensive for minors to buy cigarettes," McCaffree said.

State Question 713 was approved by voters, 53% to 47%, on November 2, 2004. The measure abolished sales tax on tobacco products, raised the cigarette tax by four cents per cigarette, and hiked taxes on other tobacco products.

The tobacco tax increase was expected to raise $200 million a year to fund a level 1 trauma center in Oklahoma City, help build and equip a cancer research center, and help fund the operations of the Oklahoma State University (OSU) College of Osteopathic Medicine in Tulsa.

In 2004, TSET was able to spend $4.4 million for the following year's programs. In August 2004, a new community-based program was unveiled with 20 grants for $75,000 each to local agencies to fight tobacco addiction. The Communities of Excellence grants program was announced by TSET chair Susan Bize. Board member Dr. George Foster said, "We were able to help communities of all sizes. Grants to smaller communities helped tremendously because they did not have resources necessary to bring together individuals and groups to combat the tobacco problem."

TSET Executive Director Strader said:

> Community groups are able to raise awareness and work with businesses, schools, and faith-based organizations. Everybody understands they have a role to play in reducing these problems that are causing us so much pain and death and disease in Oklahoma.

Attorney General Edmondson gave his support for the new TSET program for communities that became the "heart and soul" of TSET. He said, "These are the people in the trenches who have an intimate knowledge of the tobacco problem in their area. They recognize it will take us all if we whip this problem."

Communities were the key to getting the word out. Nearly every adult alive in the 21st century had a family member whose lives were cut short or quality of life reduced because of smoking and using other tobacco products.

Strader was aware the constitutional mandate for TSET went beyond tobacco cessation programs. "Once we had the basic components of a comprehensive tobacco control program in place, we were able to begin branching out into other public health programs," Strader said. "Oklahoma was near the top of the states in obesity and lack of physical activity of its citizens." Strader praised the board's strategic decision to begin funding grants and programs to address physical activity and nutrition. It was TSET's goal to use the best of available science and apply to public health programs some of the same strategies that were being used in tobacco prevention and cessation programs.

Moving from a narrow focus on tobacco into the general health of the state drew high praise later from Karla Sneegas, branch chief for the Office on Smoking and Health at the CDC:

> TSET is paving the way for what we want to think about for the future of chronic disease which is . . . maintaining the commitment to tobacco prevention and cessation, but also . . . applying that to other areas . . . such as addressing obesity and the work in nutrition and physical activity. More and more people want to see the holistic part of health addressed, not just disease specific areas.

In May 2005, Strader told reporters that nearly 10,000 tobacco users had received free help with quitting through the Oklahoma Tobacco Helpline. More than 2,400 Oklahomans called the helpline just in the month of January 2005.

> *TSET gave our state government an outlet to share valuable information with our residents about the effects of smoking and obesity. Ultimately, residents have the right to do with that knowledge what they wish, but there is no doubt that TSET has saved lives.*
>
> — OKLAHOMA CITY MAYOR DAVID HOLT

Oklahoma was praised by the Washington, D.C.-based Campaign for Tobacco-Free Kids in December 2005 as one of the most improved states for funding programs encouraging adolescents to stay away from tobacco. The state jumped from 32nd to 21st in the nation in helping youths stop smoking or never start. Janie Horton, tobacco-prevention coordinator for the Carter County Turning Point Coalition, a TSET-funded agency at the time, said, "We can help middle school students decide not to try that first cigarette. Once they start, the addiction makes it hard to quit."

50 YEARS OF LIES

On August 17, 2006, U.S. District Judge Gladys Kessler of the District of Columbia found major tobacco companies guilty of fraud and conspiracy under federal racketeering statutes in deceiving the American people about the addictive nature of nicotine and the health effects of tobacco. In the case of *United States v. Philip Morris,* Judge Kessler wrote:

> Over the course of more than 50 years, Defendants lied, misrepresented, and deceived the American public, including smokers and the young people they avidly sought as "replacement smokers" about the devastating health effects of smoking and environmental tobacco smoke.
>
> They suppressed research, they destroyed documents, they manipulated the use of nicotine so as to increase and perpetuate addiction . . . and they abused the legal system in order to achieve their goal—to make money with little, if any, regard for individual illness and suffering and soaring health costs.

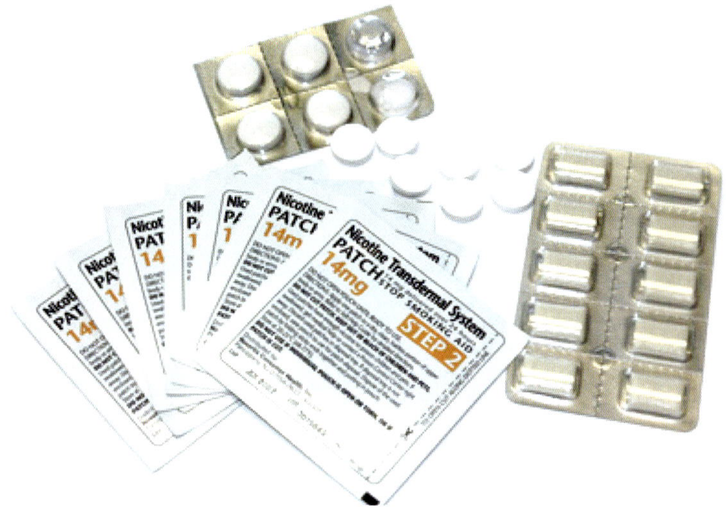

A no cost quit kit available to Oklahomans who want to live tobacco free.

A significant step for the Oklahoma Tobacco Helpline was taken in 2006 when participants were eligible to receive a free kit that contained a two-week supply of nicotine patches, gum, or lozenges, depending on each caller's needs, to help kick-start their quit attempt.

Early member of the TSET Board of Directors Casey Killblane, a former personal assistant to First Lady Barbara Bush, said the board embraced the language of the constitutional amendment that created the trust. "It was our guide and focus," she said. "We have consistently asked the question, where are we going next?"

Longtime TSET Board Member Casey Killblane.

CHAPTER TWELVE

PROTECTING THE TRUST

The legislature continually came up with ideas to try to get their hands on the trust fund. Constant reminders were needed that TSET was created by amendment to the State Constitution and could only be changed by the people.

— ATTORNEY GENERAL DREW EDMONDSON

By 2007, the TSET trust fund had increased to nearly $400 million and produced, for the first time, $10 million in annual earnings to be spent by the TSET Board of Directors. The size of the fund drew the renewed attention of legislators who wanted extra money to fund favorite programs. Much of the attention came from new members of the legislature who had been elected since the 2000 constitutional amendment and were not familiar with the restrictions or purpose of TSET.

In 2007, the legislature expanded Medicaid and looked for extra money to match federal Medicaid dollars. The last line in Senate Bill 424 by a well-meaning senator mandated that 20% of the annual TSET earnings be used for that purpose. In a committee meeting, several senators were shocked to learn that the money could not be touched without a vote of the people amending the Oklahoma Constitution.

When several additional bills were introduced in the 2007 Oklahoma legislature attempting to use TSET funds for other state government projects, Attorney General Drew Edmondson was asked by TSET Board of Directors Chairman Kenneth D. "Ken" Rowe to clarify who was in charge of TSET money.

Edmondson released an Attorney General's opinion that said "the unambiguous terms of the Constitution" give the spending responsibility to the Board of Directors of TSET, not the legislature. It was a clear signal to the legislature.

During another legislative session, it was proposed to use TSET funds to give Oklahoma public school teachers a much-deserved raise. The TSET board went on record as saying any raid of the TSET fund could erode the dramatic impact that money from the trust fund had on reducing smoking.

Also in 2007, Board of Directors Chairman Rowe was excited about the prospects of TSET helping to correct the dismal news from the CDC that Oklahoma was "dead last" in the nation in cardiovascular disease. Rowe called on every person, organization, business, and state leader to do their part in creating a "public health renaissance" by cutting tobacco use to below the national average by 2012.

Rowe, a CPA, had been appointed to the TSET board by State

Senate President Pro Tempore Cal Hobson. When Rowe asked what he was expected to do, Hobson told him, "Just do the right thing."

Dr. Robert Mannel, director of the OU Cancer Institute, proposed that TSET develop an Oklahoma Tobacco Research Center (OTRC) to identify, evaluate, and disseminate the best practices for tobacco prevention and control to reduce tobacco use and tobacco-related cancer incidence in the state. The TSET board agreed in May 2007 to provide $4 million over a five-year period to establish the OTRC, now known as the TSET Health Promotion Research Center (HPRC), under the administrative umbrella of the OU Health Stephenson Cancer Center.

TSET board member Casey Killblane reflected, "It was the first time we veered from a direct connection to reducing smoking, but we realized research was the key for the future." Killblane said the board began looking at fitness, nutrition, "the whole spectrum" of the health condition of Oklahomans.

Oklahoma was positioned to bring new cessation research to the rest of the country. Tobacco use and cessation programs continued to evolve.

The plan was for OTRC to be a statewide collaboration including researchers from institutions throughout the state. The OTRC would establish partnerships with TSET-funded and OSDH-funded tobacco control programs.

The mission of OTRC, now HPRC, is to reduce the burden of disease in the state by addressing modifiable health risk factors

OTRC
OKLAHOMA TOBACCO RESEARCH CENTER
PEGGY AND CHARLES STEPHENSON OKLAHOMA CANCER CENTER

such as tobacco use, sedentary lifestyle, poor diet, and risky use of alcohol and other substances.

Recognizing the need to develop media campaigns to encourage Oklahomans to call the Tobacco Helpline, the TSET board partnered with OSDH to develop an ad campaign. Focus groups reviewed radio, television, and print ads for effectiveness. TSET continued to use the services of Dr. Laura Beebe at the OU College of Public Health to develop an evaluation design to assess a change in attitude among those who encountered the anti-smoking and tobacco use messages.

TSET partnered with the National Alliance for Tobacco Cessation (NATC) beginning in 2007. The partnership assured the Oklahoma Tobacco Helpline reached thousands more people each year.

In 2009, Oklahoma moved up to number 11 among the states in funding programs to prevent minors from taking up smoking and to help existing smokers quit. There was other good news. The adult smoking rate had dropped from 28.7 the previous year to 24.7%. It was the first time since statistics were kept that less than one-quarter of Oklahoma adults smoked. In addition, more than 37,000 Oklahomans called the Oklahoma Tobacco Helpline in 2009.

Also in 2009, the Oklahoma Hospital Association (OHA) partnered with TSET with a grant called Hospitals Helping Patients Quit. The focus was to help Oklahoma hospitals implement an evidence-based tobacco treatment system for patients. Joy Leuthard, the new OHA manager of health improvement initiatives, used TSET grant money to hire OHA staff to help hospitals develop a smooth system to refer patients directly to the Oklahoma Tobacco Helpline.

The OHA program has assisted more than 25,000 Oklahoma hospital patients to get help to end their addiction. Leuthard reflected, "This would not have happened without TSET. The grants were the impetus for infrastructure changes in hospitals."

By 2010, the TSET fund balance was $488 million. With an annual budget of more than $20 million from earnings, the TSET board heard presentations from three different Oklahoma entities that used adult stem cell research in the fight against cancer. Board member Killblane remembered that fellow board members were surprised that so much stem cell research was going on in the state.

It was suggested that perhaps the three research groups work together. It was a brilliant idea that led to the creation of the Oklahoma Center for Adult Stem Cell Research Center (OCASCR), a collaboration between OU and OSU and housed at the Oklahoma Medical Research Foundation. The TSET board voted to give $5.5 million over five years to create OCASCR.

OCASCR promotes research into the promise of adult stem cell biology to develop treatments for a range of chronic medical conditions, including cancer. OCASCR has brought many world-recognized investigators to Oklahoma to conduct research in

THE SECRET SAUCE

Ken Rowe, who in 2025 is the longest-serving member of the TSET Board of Directors, has witnessed board members aligning beyond personal agendas when making decisions as a board. Rowe said, "I think that's part of the secret sauce why the board has worked so well together."

TSET changed the culture of Oklahoma which had one of the strongest tobacco cultures in the nation. We helped create a fund with a vision, with a purpose, with a goal to improve the health of Oklahoma, a fund that will be there long after my grandchildren are gone.

— DR. ROBERT McCAFFREE

stem cells and regenerative medicine, a field that strives to restore the normal functions of cells, tissues, and organs that have been damaged by disease.

TSET played a significant role in the opening of the OU Stephenson Cancer Center (SCC) in Oklahoma City in 2011. Charles and Peggy Stephenson of Antlers and Tulsa donated $12 million as part of a $50 million private fundraising campaign.

THE VALUE OF RESEARCH

Medical research is the best chance we have to improve the quality of life for our children and grandchildren. It's a longer-term play, with no guarantees. But on the other hand, when a big breakthrough comes through, it will impact our entire state. TSET is committed to research.

— KEN ROWE

Later, the Stephenson family gave another $20 million to expand the SCC research mission.

Inside the SCC, TSET funded ongoing research in tobacco-related cancer deaths. At the time, the death rate from cancer was more than 30% higher in Oklahoma than any other state. The TSET Phase I Clinical Trials Center at SCC recruited cancer researchers called "Oklahoma TSET Cancer Research Scholars." In addition, TSET funding was used to leverage other funding to establish and expand core services at SCC, the OU Health Sciences Center, the Oklahoma Medical Research Foundation, and the Helmerich Research Center at OSU-Tulsa.

In 2011, Dr. Beebe reported that TSET's programs, policy, and media campaigns all influenced anti-tobacco norms within Oklahoma. She credited Communities of Excellence grants in leading the way in the state being able to reduce tobacco consumption by a billion cigarettes.

The TSET Board of Directors, with the help of consultant Frank W. Merrick of Foundation Management Inc., held a brainstorming conference in 2011 with groups sponsored by TSET and with stakeholders in the Oklahoma health care and tobacco prevention community. It was the board's idea to move to "the next level" of cessation and prevention programs and general health initiatives.

Tulsa CPA Don Millican was appointed to the TSET Board of Directors by State Treasurer Ken Miller in 2012. Millican and other board members developed a policy to place a portion of annual payments in reserve to be used in future years. He said, "Because of the up and down trends in investment earnings, it was important that we have money to continue worthy grants or programs in years in which our investment income was low or negative." With a fiscally responsible policy in place, Millican said, "You can have a year where you had a disaster in the market, but you still have a payout to grantees."

Don Millican became a TSET board member in 2012.

By 2012, TSET funded 49 urban and rural coalitions through the Communities of Excellence program, creating daily conversations about healthy choices across the state. Thousands of youth participated in local Students Working Against Tobacco (SWAT) teams. In Lawton, more than 120 teenagers inspired their peers to say "no" to tobacco. That caught the attention of national media.

From 2002 to 2011, high school smoking in Oklahoma dropped from 24 to 17.8%. And for the first time, there were more former smokers than current smokers in Oklahoma.

TSET-sponsored programs also worked with local school boards to make schools in southeastern Oklahoma tobacco free. That was a major win because Pushmataha, Choctaw, and McCurtain counties had the highest adult smoking rates in the state.

In 2013, Dr. McCaffree reported on the impact that TSET grants were having on tobacco research in the state. He noted that Dr. Laura Beebe was the only tobacco researcher in Oklahoma when TSET first established the OTRC in 2008. Just five years later, 125 research team members in 15 institutions were on board. The TSET grants of nearly $3.7 million were "extremely successful" in allowing the institutions to at least double the available funds to hire researchers and staff. TSET authorized another $20 million over five years for OTRC at the Stephenson Cancer Center. The existence of that research wing contributed to Stephenson being the only cancer center in Oklahoma certified by the National Cancer Institute (NCI).

Julie Bisbee was hired by TSET in 2012 as the Public Information and Outreach Officer. She was a former journalist for the Associated Press and *The Oklahoman.* She was policy director for the Oklahoma Institute for Child Advocacy when she joined TSET.

Also in 2013, the TSET board approved the recruitment of 42 physicians over four years through the Oklahoma Medical Loan Repayment program. The goal was to assist the Oklahoma Health Care Workforce Training Commission to pay a new doctor's medical school loans if the doctor committed to practice in a rural or underserved area of the state for four years.

At the same time, TSET expanded its grants to communities and schools. The Healthy Community Incentive Grants and Healthy Schools Incentive Grants were awarded to communities, school districts, and individual schools that passed proven policies to reduce tobacco use and improve health. Former TSET board chair Jim Gebhart reflected, "It is worthwhile when TSET is able

> *The designation of Stephenson Cancer Center in 2018 as a National Cancer Institute center would not have happened without TSET.*
>
> — DR. ROBERT MANNEL
>
> DIRECTOR, STEPHENSON CANCER CENTER

I was asked once why I was on the TSET board. I'm not a doctor or scientist, but I'm a mom. There are a whole bunch of moms in this state and the health of our children is important.

— CASEY KILLBLANE

to help schools, especially elementary schools, with programs that assist them in educating our youth about the harmful effects of tobacco use."

Tracey Strader retired as executive director of TSET at the end of 2016. Her replacement was John Woods, the former president and CEO of the Norman Chamber of Commerce. He also had been on the staff of Congressman Tom Cole. Strader looked back on her 17 years as director of TSET with pride and still believed in the choice of Oklahomans:

The beauty of this endowment strategy is that it's in perpetuity. That means until the end of time. We will be

Members of the Jenks Public Schools Board of Education acknowledge a TSET Health Schools Incentive grant.

Three strong TSET supporters in 2015. From left, former Attorney General Drew Edmondson, Commissioner of Mental Health and Substance Abuse Terry Cline, and State Senator Ben Robinson.

Oklahoma City Thunder star Kevin Durant helped celebrate the 15th anniversary of TSET in 2015.

TSET HEALTHY INCENTIVE PROGRAM
COMMUNITIES

here fighting the fight against tobacco, trying to improve the health of Oklahomans for generations to come.

Dr. Beebe of the OU Health Sciences Center and researchers at the University of Wisconsin School of Medicine and Public Health released a study in January 2017 that showed that adult smoking rates in Oklahoma were plunging 10 times faster than smoking rates in comparable states. The study credited TSET grants and programs as being "primarily responsible" for the state's rapid decline. The study also said Oklahoma had 126,000 fewer smokers than 11 years before. Dr. Beebe said, "This comprehensive, sustained approach is clearly making a difference, saving lives, and reducing the burden of tobacco on Oklahoma."

In 2017, state government faced an $868 million shortfall, prompting a member of the House of Representatives to prefile a bill to take half of TSET's earnings each year to allocate to public school districts to promote the health and quality of life for students. Immediately, House staff members informed the bill's author what had been the law for 17 years—the legislature could not decide how to spend TSET money.

Even with a heavy emphasis on reducing tobacco use and significant progress in that area, we still have a long way to go. Too many of our young people are becoming addicted. Too many smokers have not yet managed to quit. Too many Oklahomans are still breathing secondhand smoke in workplaces and public places.

— GOVERNOR MARY FALLIN

The Oklahoma Council on Public Affairs (OCPA) wanted to use TSET funds to alleviate the budget crisis. The group called on the legislature to use TSET funds to protect core services otherwise funded by legislative appropriations. Director Woods wrote a letter to the editor that pointed out that OCPA for many years had received significant funding from the parent company of Marlboro. Woods wrote, "OCPA's recent actions show that the 'think tank' has accepted the role of dutiful protector for Big Tobacco's agenda."

There was again great interest in the corpus of the trust which had grown to more than $1 billion. A House Joint Resolution was also filed to ask voters to amend the Oklahoma Constitution so that future payments from the tobacco companies would not go to TSET. Instead, the money would be directed to a new Oklahoma Rural Health Care Infrastructure Fund. The governing board of that fund would devote investment earnings to various health care causes in rural areas.

The Oklahoman's editorial page noted that both measures were passed by House committees but, "Neither should advance further. TSET has worked well for years. There's no need to 'fix' it." Neither the joint resolution nor the bill were ever heard by the full House of Representatives.

In the 2018 legislative session, State Representative Harold Wright of Weatherford authored a bill to prohibit smoking in indoor public places, including bars, and in all enclosed areas where Oklahomans work. State Labor Commissioner Leslie Osborn endorsed the bill, noting that tobacco companies were spending $174 million a year on advertising in Oklahoma plus what they paid their lobbyists. Osborn said, "It's time for us to stand up and talk to our representatives and senators about standing up to them."

Because of strong opposition from tobacco lobbyists, Wright's bill failed to advance. One observer said, "Same song, different verse."

At the time, Oklahoma was one of only three states that still allowed smoking in bars. Of the 30 cities with an NBA team, Oklahoma City was one of five that did not have 100% smoke-free restaurants and bars.

In January 2019, TSET board chair Dr. Bruce Benjamin appointed board members Casey Killblane and Michelle Stephens to join him on an executive search committee to screen candidates for a new executive director after Woods resigned.

Past TSET Board Chairman Marshall Snipes and Dr. Bruce Benjamin at the Southern Obesity Summit in Oklahoma City.

Julie Bisbee was named interim director in December 2018, managing and representing the agency with the legislature. On March 28, 2019, Bisbee was unanimously approved by the board as the TSET Executive Director.

At the board meeting at which Bisbee was appointed interim director, Marshall Snipes was a new member, the appointee of Oklahoma Attorney General Mike Hunter. Snipes had heard from others that TSET "needed more scrutiny." Over the next few months, Snipes found just the opposite. He said:

> I discovered the agency had been well run since inception. Julie had reenergized the staff and began to mold the strategic plan to put TSET in a position to be successful for many years to come.
>
> Instead of finding a state agency with major issues and in need of reform, I found a well-run agency that is an example of how government should work . . . dedicated employees, effective programs, low overhead, and an engaged board.

CHAPTER THIRTEEN

A MODEL FOR THE NATION

As time passed, Oklahoma's TSET became a national model for ensuring tobacco settlement funds were spent to reduce the toll of tobacco. It showed great wisdom to preserve the money so we would have it for future generations.

— FORMER GOVERNOR MARY FALLIN

Both the governor and the legislature had their eyes on the $1.3 billion TSET trust fund in 2020. In his state of the state message, Governor Kevin Stitt recommended that future TSET money be directed toward improving delivery of health care in rural Oklahoma.

In the first few weeks of the 2020 legislative session, the State Senate Rules Committee approved Senate Joint Resolution 27 by State Senator Kim David of Porter. The resolution called for a vote of the people to amend the Oklahoma Constitution to reduce TSET's share of the annual money from tobacco companies from 75 to 25%. The legislature would receive the remainder to match federal money for an expanded Medicaid program.

State Senator Greg McCortney's bill, Senate Joint Resolution 28, was also approved by the Rules Committee. It would allow TSET to spend its annual payment immediately, rather than the money going into the trust fund. He suggested it would free up another $50 million a year for the legislature to appropriate.

Former Attorney General Edmondson spoke out in opposition to any adverse changes to TSET. He pointed to the constitutional amendment passed by voters 20 years before. He told the *Tulsa World*, "They did not want the legislature controlling this money and they wanted it spent on public health." Edmondson was aware that the state needed money to help fund Medicaid but said lawmakers had other revenue sources. He said, "They can restore cuts made to the gross production tax and income tax. TSET is working and benefitting people and should not be starved.

Several public health groups criticized the legislature's attempt to overhaul TSET funding. The American Heart Association, American Cancer Society, American Lung Association, and the Campaign for Tobacco-Free Kids said redirecting TSET funds would have a "devastating" effect on Oklahoma's public health. A joint statement said:

> Smoking continues to be the No. 1 cause of preventable death in Oklahoma and is responsible for 31% of the state's cancer deaths. TSET is the state's primary source of tobacco control and prevention funding. The trust also provides crucial access to healthcare.

The legislature completed action on Senate Joint Resolution 27 which was scheduled to appear as State Question 814 on the general election ballot on November 3, 2020. The joint resolution was one of very few bills passed by the 2020 legislature. The COVID-19 pandemic caused legislators to leave the Capitol for three weeks. Then, only legislators and Capitol employees were allowed in the building.

Governor Stitt endorsed the state question. He said, "We need to direct some of those funds to the legislature so we can actually pay for Medicaid expansion." The governor had opposed Medicaid expansion which won approval by state voters a few months before.

TSET spokesman Thomas Larson told a reporter, "Smaller payments going into the trust could reduce the agency's ability to fund future initiatives. With less money going into the endowment, the fund will not grow as quickly, especially when we have a downturn in the economy."

A broad coalition led by the American Cancer Society Cancer Action Network (ACS-CAN), the American Heart Association, the Americans for Nonsmokers' Rights Foundation and the Campaign for Tobacco-Free Kids educated voters on the public health advances in Oklahoma because of TSET. The health organizations opposed changes to TSET's funding structure.

"Protecting TSET *and* funding Medicaid expansion will save Oklahomans' lives and money," said Matt Glanville, government relations director at ACS-CAN. "Big Tobacco spends over $170 million a year in marketing their addictive products in Oklahoma. This is the wrong time to divest in the fight against their deadline products."

Sarah Riven, government relations director for the Oklahoma Chapter of the American Heart Association, expressed her group's opposition. She said, "Approval of the question will prove costly to future generations. TSET is one thing that Oklahoma has done very well. We need to protect those dollars going to TSET at all costs."

On election day, voters overwhelmingly rejected the state question by more than a quarter million votes, 58.8% to 41.2%. The state question was rejected by voters in all 77 counties. TSET Board Chair Marshall Snipes said, "The citizens of Oklahoma continue to support TSET, its programs and its funding, independent from the legislature and the governor."

As the TSET corpus grew, more people credited Oklahoma with "doing it right" with its share of the tobacco settlement money. Peter Fisher, vice president of the Campaign for Tobacco-Free Kids, agreed. He said, "I hear people in other states say, 'We wish we could have done something like

Thomas Larson helped celebrate the 20th anniversary of the Oklahoma Tobacco Helpline.

Oklahoma has done.'" Fisher said that legislatures in many of the states that did not protect their money in a trust have spent their allotted amount, especially those states that securitized the settlement money for upfront cash. The tobacco money was "long gone" and anti-smoking efforts took back seat to legislative priorities of roads, bridges, and other state government projects.

"Those states thought only about the short-term," TSET Board Chair Michelle Stephens said.

Stephens applauded the TSET board for its 2020 passage of the Healthy Youth Initiative as TSET's commitment to roll out new programs aimed at young Oklahomans. A new media campaign warned teens of the dangers of tobacco use and vaping, while a new text-based service, My Life, My Quit, offered cessation support to teens already addicted to nicotine. In the fall of 2021, the Youth Action for Health Leadership (YAHL) began recruiting students to take a health leadership role in their communities. A TSET grant to the Oklahoma State Department of Education helped fund teacher training and certification in health education.

Beyond TSET's work, Stephens noted that legislative action could accelerate changes sought by TSET's efforts to prevent and reduce tobacco addiction in youth and improve health:

- The passage of a comprehensive smoke-free air law
- Give cities and towns the power to create their own tobacco regulation
- Provide more safe and convenient places for physical activity such as parks and sidewalks
- Make it easier for residents to be near to a grocery store selling fresh fruits and vegetables

Secondhand smoke continued to be a concern for TSET as thousands of Oklahomans were exposed to secondhand smoke in their workplaces. Bars, casinos, and restaurants employed more than 200,000 employees. Many of those workers are not protected by clean indoor air laws because of loopholes in state law. Oklahoma is one of only two states that lack a comprehensive clean air law and still prohibit cities and towns from passing strict tobacco control measures at the local level.

Even though polls continued to show nearly 80% of Oklahomans favored a statewide ban on smoking in eating, drinking, and gambling establishments, the pervasive influence of Big Tobacco has so far prevented the Sooner State from being on the cutting edge of anti-smoking public policy.

Another legislative attempt was made in 2023 to control investments of the TSET trust fund. House Bill 2254 would require the TSET Board of Investors to invest 4% of the endowment in Oklahoma-based venture capital entities. The bill passed the House of Representatives 54-37. However, the bill failed to receive a hearing in the Senate Appropriations Committee.

In March 2024, TSET launched two new media messages aimed at teenage tobacco prevention and cessation—"What Finally Worked" from My Life, My Quit and "The Difference Shows" from the rural-focused Down and Dirty campaign. Both campaigns were based on real Oklahoma teens dealing with the vaping epidemic. My Life, My Quit was promoted to connect teens 13–17 who vape or used tobacco with personalized live texting, phone, and web chat support.

"Media campaigns are not like they were 20 years ago," said TSET's Thomas Larson highlighting how the campaign uses social media platforms including Instagram, Snapchat, Facebook, and YouTube to reach its target audience.

The message was that using e-cigarettes and vaping were also dangerous. Larson said, "It's not a harmless activity. Vaping aerosols have heavy metals in them." The fear is that if youngsters start vaping, they are more likely to move on to use traditional tobacco products in their adult years.

The focus on anti-vaping was timely because of trends in Oklahoma. In 2022, 21.7% of Oklahoma high school students vaped, compared to a national rate of 14.1%. However, the 2022 figure had dropped six percentage points from 2021. The fact

THE TOLL OF TOBACCO IN OKLAHOMA

- 7,500 adults die each year from their own smoking
- Smoking kills more people than alcohol, AIDS, auto accidents, illegal drugs, murders, and suicides combined
- Annual health care costs directly caused by smoking—$1.88 billion
- Annual Medicaid costs caused by smoking—$283.8 million
- Each household pays $1,057 annually for tax burden from smoking-caused government expenditures
- Annual productivity loss caused by smoking—$4.6 billion
- 4% of high school students who smoke (national rate 1.9%)
- 21.7% of high school students who use e-cigarettes (national rate 10%)
- 15.6% of adults who smoke (national rate 11.6%)
- An estimated $148.9 million spent by tobacco companies on advertising in Oklahoma (nationwide $8.6 billion)

Source: 2024, www.tobaccofreekids.org

that one-fifth of high school students in the state vaped troubled TSET board members. TSET Exectutive Director Julie Bisbee said, "We are focused on educating people about the dangers of vaping through grants to organizations that work with retailers to inform them about the state law that tobacco and vaping products can only be sold to people who are 21 or older."

In April 2024, TSET's Healthy Youth Initiative, through its Swap Up brand, won two honors at the NYX Awards, an international marketing and creative idea competition. Swap Up, an obesity prevention campaign aimed at teens in the state, won two Gold Awards. Bisbee said, "These awards underscore TSET's commitment to creativity and innovation in empowering Oklahoma teens to make healthy choices." One version of the message geared to youth in metro areas and the other aimed for rural Oklahoma teens explained how water can improve concentration and focus while sugar-sweetened drinks can cause an energy crash.

From the time the first TSET grant was made, evaluation has been an integral part of each program and initiative. Information contained in the TSET annual report documents the success or failure of each effort as part of the overall goal of creating a healthier Oklahoma.

Don Millican, a longtime member of the TSET Board of Directors, had advice for future board members:

> Never take your foot off the accelerator. TSET has made a massive difference in smoking and tobacco use. There will be people who live a lot longer and are healthier because of TSET. Now, vaping and obesity are logical targets for the future. The wisdom of the voters in 2000 gave TSET the flexibility to meet the demands of change on the health care horizon.

Former chairs of the TSET Board, front row, from left Runako Whittaker, Suzanna Gattoni, Michelle Stephens, and Marshall Snipes. Back row Bruce Benjamin and Jack Allen.

Oklahoma Congressman Tom Cole, third from left, was a guest at the OU Health Stephenson Cancer Center. From left, Casey Killblane, Don Millican, Curtis Knoles, Ken Rowe, and Bruce Benjamin.

From left, Marshall Snipes, Julie Bisbee, and Jerome Loughridge.

CHAPTER FOURTEEN

REAPING THE REWARDS—THE RESULTS

Statewide comprehensive tobacco control programs that are sustained over time have been shown to work: they reduce smoking rates, tobacco-related diseases and deaths, protect people from secondhand smoke exposure, encourage smokers to quit, and prevent youth from starting in the first place.

— DR. TIM MCAFEE, DIRECTOR OF THE OFFICE ON SMOKING AND HEALTH, CENTERS FOR DISEASE CONTROL AND PREVENTION, BEST PRACTICES FOR COMPREHENSIVE TOBACCO CONTROL, 2014

When the TSET Board of Directors funded its first program, there were few models on how to effectively prevent and reduce tobacco use. But the goals were clear—keep people from starting, help people quit, and protect people from toxic secondhand smoke.

TSET Executive Director Tracey Strader, second from left, and former Board Members, from left, Brian Maddy, Susan Walters, and Dr. Robert McCaffree celebrate the 15th anniversary of TSET.

If these goals were met, Oklahoma could expect to reduce tobacco use, save lives, and save money—and TSET made good on that promise.

"We chose programs that we thought could get the most bang for the buck," said founding board member Susan Walters Bize. "One of the first was the Oklahoma Tobacco Helpline. It would have statewide impact and give people the opportunity to call and get a counselor who could help them stop."

By 2008, the TSET Board of Directors accumulated enough earnings from the endowment to fund the elements of a comprehensive tobacco control program—a statewide tobacco cessation helpline, community-based grants, and counter marketing campaigns.

SAVING LIVES, SAVING MONEY

In 2023, the North American Quitline Consortium ranked the Oklahoma Tobacco Helpline as the best in the country for

reaching tobacco users in need of treatment. In 2024, the Helpline served more than 27,270 Oklahomans and had a 44% quit rate—the benchmark is 30%.

Also in 2024, the Helpline celebrated a milestone of 20 years of free tobacco cessation services to Oklahomans. During that time, the Oklahoma Tobacco Helpline has received over 590,000 registrations. Of those, nearly 13,000 were women who were pregnant, postpartum, or considering pregnancy.

In addition, TSET has funded grants with the Oklahoma Health Care Authority which administers the state's Medicaid program to ensure access to tobacco cessation services, targeting vulnerable populations such as pregnant women and identifying health risks such as obesity and tobacco use.

- About 15% of costs of the state Medicaid program pays for the cost of treating smoking-related health conditions. TSET is the primary source of funding for a statewide program to prevent and reduce tobacco use and provide tobacco cessation services.
- From FY2017–FY2023 it is estimated that the Oklahoma Medicaid program saved $19.9 million in hospital costs by Medicaid members receiving services from the Oklahoma Tobacco Helpline.
- $157.4 million in savings are estimated to be realized when Medicaid members quit smoking. Of those savings $33.1 million in savings was attributable to Medicaid smokers who quit by using the Oklahoma Tobacco Helpline.

With a multifaceted approach, TSET grants, programs, and innovation are changing lives. TSET's work with health systems ensures opportunities for tobacco-free lifestyles. Infusing tobacco cessation and wellness into systems is a proven practice to help ensure all Oklahomans have access.

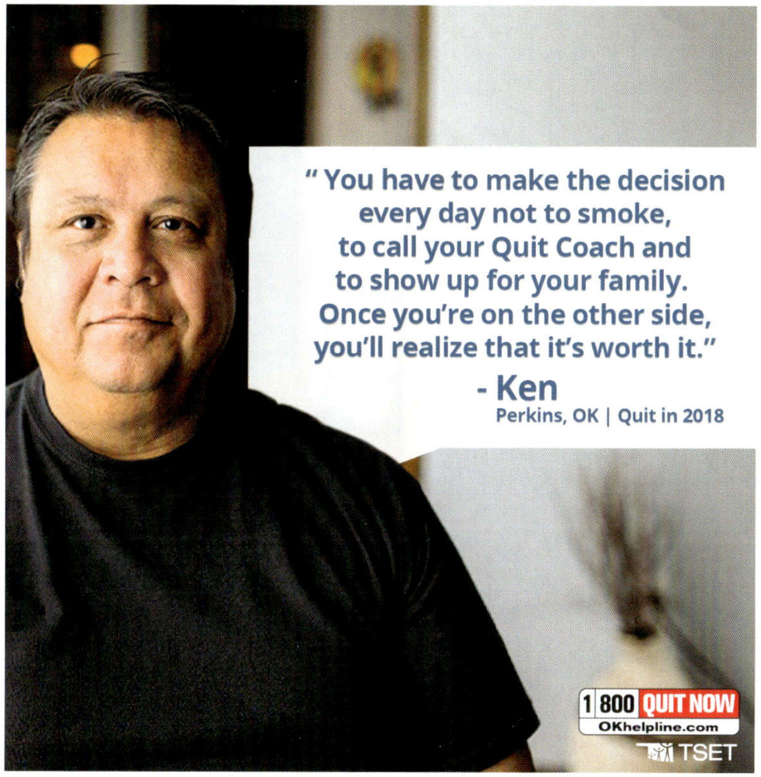

WorkHealthy HOSPITALS

Over the years, TSET's work has focused on Oklahomans who have a higher rate of tobacco use and death. Rates of smoking are 2 to 4 times higher among people with psychiatric and substance abuse disorders. TSET partners with the Oklahoma Department of Mental Health and Substance Abuse Services to promote tobacco cessation, tobacco-free environments, and encourage physical activity and improved nutrition. The state's services for mental health and substance abuse treatment have referred more than 47,000 people to the Oklahoma Tobacco Helpline since 2016. In addition, work on health promoting policies at seven facilities has reached more than 94,500 consumers each year.

TSET's partnership with the Oklahoma Hospital Association helps hospitals make improvements to health policies and environments. The program acknowledges that employees in medical facilities are often community role models for health. More than 75 hospitals have committed to participating in health improvement programs that support employee wellness, tobacco cessation for patients and TSET's work with OHA also ensure workers are trained and ready to support patients in their efforts to quit tobacco.

Through OHA's Health Improvement Initiatives, outpatient clinics and hospitals significantly increased patient referrals to the Oklahoma Tobacco Helpline. Some years, as many as 54,000 patients might be referred to the Oklahoma Tobacco Helpline for services.

Thanks to sustained and strategic investments in preventing and reducing tobacco use, Oklahoma is outpacing its peer states in the rate of reduction of smokers in states that have similar clean indoor air laws and tax structures. A study of Oklahoma's work to prevent and reduce tobacco compared to peer states in 2018, showed that the smoking rate in Oklahoma had decreased ten times faster than the peer group.

The study by OU Health Sciences Center for Tobacco Research and Intervention at the University of Wisconsin School of

A SUCCESS STORY

"I had a heart attack, all alone, in my apartment. I was scared, obviously, because I shouldn't be in my early 30s and almost dying. So, I did quit smoking. And then turned around and went right back. Tobacco is tough. One day, my son found my cigar wrappers, and he said to me, 'Dad, you need to quit. I want you to quit." When my doctor told me about the Oklahoma Tobacco Helpline, it opened up a new door. This time, I had people in my corner supporting me — which I didn't expect. They were so encouraging, and they still are to this day. I couldn't have done this by myself."

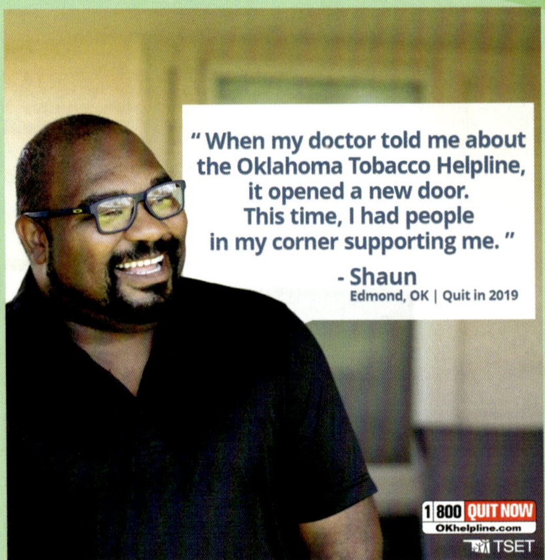

"Since quitting tobacco, it's been exciting! I took up running two miles daily and a new healthier diet in 2021. So far, I've lost 63 pounds and completed my first 5k! I would be untruthful if I said I haven't had cravings or thought hard about smoking since I quit in 2019. However, the Oklahoma Tobacco Helpline is still the greatest resource I carry with me everywhere I go. Having that support at my fingertips over the last almost 2½ years has changed my life!"

— SHAUN IN EDMOND

Medicine and Public Health showed sustained investment in best practice tobacco use and cessation was paying off.

TSET's ability to fund grants and programs over time coupled with sustained investment in community programs and mass media efforts yielded results that other states were not seeing. Peer states included Alabama, Arkansas, Colorado, Idaho, Louisiana, and Tennessee. The states shared similar sales tax and excise tax laws.

TSET's programs also focus on lasting change. Keeping young people from starting was key to reducing the number

Because of TSET, Oklahoma
SMOKING RATES HAVE DROPPED 10X FASTER
than similar states.

Smoking among kids

CUT IN HALF.

of adult smokers. Hard-hitting media campaigns, community-based grants, and local efforts to create more smokefree and tobacco free environments were helping to reinforce a smokefree future.

In 2019, youth smoking dropped to single digits for the first time, according to the Youth Risk Behavior Survey. With only 9.1% of Oklahomans under the age of 18 smoking cigarettes TSET celebrated progress.

INVESTING IN THE FUTURE

At the same time, the rate of youth vaping and young people experimenting with vapor products was increasing. To meet that need, the TSET Board of Directors launched the TSET Healthy Youth Initiative which began with public education campaigns aimed at informing young people of the harms of vapor products. Research studies show that young people are two-times more likely to be influenced to smoke by cigarette marketing than by peer pressure.

"Changing behaviors and preventing chronic disease are key to improving the health of Oklahomans, and healthy behaviors learning early last into adulthood," said Michelle Stephens, board member. "Creating a healthier future for Oklahoma starts with today's youth."

Additional phases of the initiative included a statewide youth advocacy program. Youth Action for Health Leadership (YAHL) works to empower high school students to be leaders for health improvement. Successful Futures focuses on ensuring younger students grades three through eight learn about healthy choices.

Public education efforts for youth hit the mark. Survey results showed teens who interacted with the Swap Up campaign shifted their attitudes, beliefs and behaviors around nutrition. More than 80 percent of teens who had interacted with Swap Up campaigns online, by either watching ads or clicking campaign links to the Swap Up website, believed drinking more water would help them think more clearly, improve their mood, and perform better in school sports. Teens who are aware of Swap Up were 15% more likely to have consumed fruit and 21% more likely to have consumed vegetables in the past 7 days, compared to those who had not been exposed to the campaign.

PROMOTING HEALTH

Counter-marketing campaigns are among the most powerful tools for promoting healthy choices and supporting behavior change.

TSET Healthy Youth Initiative

It is a recommended practice by the Centers for Disease Control and Prevention. TSET has consistently used public education to counter the marketing efforts of the tobacco industry, which spends roughly $148.9 million in Oklahoma each year, according to the Campaign for Tobacco Free Kids.

Through TSET's investment in public health messaging, Oklahomans can more effectively weigh glitzy, for-profit marketing against accurate information about healthy choices.

TSET's public education programs such as Tobacco Stops With Me and Shape Your Future help Oklahomans make better decisions to improve their health.

Shape your future

Since 2008, Tobacco Stops With Me has educated on the negative effects and impact of tobacco, including nicotine addiction and secondhand smoke. Hard-hitting ads and campaigns have shown to increase knowledge of deceptive tobacco industry practices and the need for improved policy in Oklahoma.

Helping Oklahomans adopt and maintain a healthy lifestyle is the goal of the Shape Your Future public education campaign. The award-winning campaign and website educate Oklahomans on ways to eat better, move more, drink water, and be tobacco free. Evaluations of the campaign show that people who see the ads are more likely to make healthier choices, like drinking water. Parents and caregivers also show increased knowledge of the importance of healthy choices for their children.

"These health communication campaigns have been used, at very little cost by other states and even nationally," said Sjonna Paulson, who directed the strategic communication work for more than 15 years. "Not only have these campaigns racked up scholarly credentials, but the campaigns have also won more than 100 awards since 2008, including four Heartland Emmy nominations, two national Telly awards and dozens of local and regional awards."

CREATING HEALTHIER COMMUNITIES

TSET has consistently worked within communities to promote positive health change to prevent and reduce tobacco use and

A TSET innovative grant helped develop a walking trail at Champlin Park in Enid.

Development of walking trails were the focus of a TSET grant in Muskogee.

obesity. Through grant programs like Communities of Excellence and the TSET Healthy Living Program, local organizations brought forth change. Early work by the Communities of Excellence program yielded tobacco free schools. TSET Healthy Living Program focused on sectors and hot spots as the programs worked to reduce health disparities. Through the first wave of the TSET Healthy Living Program, more than 1,200 tobacco-free policies and 1,000 wellness policies were adopted helping to improve the lives of millions of Oklahomans and prompting important policy changes.

Ensuring access to quality medical care is also key in creating healthy communities. Thanks to TSET's partnership with the Oklahoma Health Care Workforce Training Commission (HWTC), formerly known as the Physician

From left, TSET Executive Director Julie Bisbee, Oklahoma City Mayor David Holt, and TSET Board Member Casey Killblane at the Southern Obesity Summit.

In 2015, TSET provided the first in-person training sessions for Healthy Living Program grantees.

Manpower Training Commission, residents are getting better access to care.

HWTC's Physician Loan Repayment Program is a public/private partnership that repays a physician's medical school loans in exchange for service in an underserved area for up to four years. After completing the program, more than half of TSET-sponsored physicians remained working in rural areas.

TSET provides 40% of funding, with state, community, or federal dollars picking up the rest. TSET began partnering with HWTC in 2013 and has sponsored more than 100 physicians, including the 42 who are currently in the program. In 2024, doctors saw more than 114,000 patients, including 23,000 Medicaid-insured Oklahomans. Since the program began, physicians in the program have provided nearly 670,000 patient visits, including 175,000 Medicaid patient visits.

INCENTIVE GRANTS — REWARDING ACHIEVEMENTS IN HEALTH

Acknowledging the role schools and communities can have in impacting daily choices for health, TSET has provided incentive grants for schools and communities that adopt health-promoting policies and strategies. Grant funds, often leveraged with dollars for other organizations, have helped to build basketball courts, walking trails, purchase playground equipment, and provide much needed opportunities for physical activity. TSET has awarded more than $9 million in incentive grants since 2012.

In 2015, the City of Muskogee received a Healthy Incentive grant.

The City of Lawton was the recipient of a $180,000 Healthy Incentive grant.

The Town of Meeker received a TSET Healthy Incentive Grant in 2021 for the construction of a new playground.

Town leaders in Taft with a mock-up of a check for a TSET Healthy Incentive Grant for a playground for children.

TSET awarded a Healthy Incentive Grant to Grove Public Schools for outdoor recreation equipment.

To help create healthy communities TSET has also invested in grants to promote healthy lifestyles and reduce risk factors for preventable disease. Grants awarded to universities, cities, and towns have helped to create outdoor recreation areas—publicly accessible pickleball courts in Alva; transformations of a botanic garden at Oklahoma State University; and sidewalk and parks projects in communities across the state.

DISCOVERY GRANTS

TSET Discovery Grants fund emerging opportunities to partner with organizations to improve the health and lives of Oklahomans. The three-year grants are aimed at immediate, impactful programs relating to tobacco cessation and prevention, health care access, senior health, and improving the overall health of all Oklahomans. The Discovery Grants allowed TSET to partner for innovation and grow the strength of organizations working to improve health.

CONNECTING FOR HEALTH

Project ECHO, a program designed to improve health care in rural areas, helps bring new education, resources, and connection to doctors and other leaders across the state. TSET's partnership with Oklahoma State University Center for Health Sciences supports videoconferencing with experts and workers across the state. TSET's funding supports curriculum for diabetes management in schools, healthy nutrition for student athletes, support for community health workers, and pediatric psychiatry, among others.

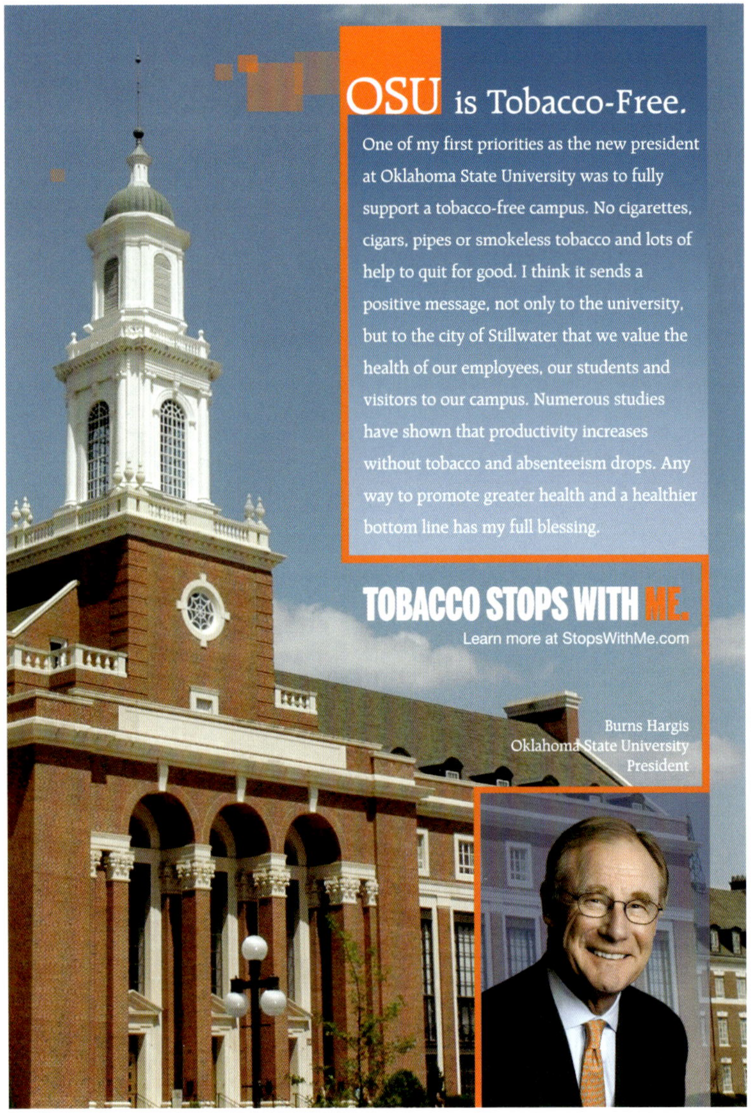

Oklahoma State University President V. Burns Hargis led the effort to make the OSU campus in Stillwater tobacco-free.

Working to increase access, especially in rural areas, is in line with TSET's strategy to reduce risk factors for cancer and heart disease. Through a partnership with Hunger Free Oklahoma, more farmers markets are accepting food stamps and people receiving nutritional assistance can purchase more fruits and vegetables. The Double Up Oklahoma (DUO) program in Oklahoma also supports a change in systems used in stores. This has become a model for the nation. In the first three years of the partnership, DUO worked with 114,000 unique Oklahomans using food stamps and issued more than 1.5 million fruit and vegetable vouchers and redeemed about 600,000.

Ensuring access to fresh fruit and vegetables is key to increasing fruit and vegetable consumption. TSET and Oklahoma State University are working together on a project to stock the shelves of foodbanks with fresh produce from the OSU Student Farm.

By collaborating and expanding relationships with community partners such as Our Daily Bread Food and Resource Center as well as the Regional Food Bank of Oklahoma, the project aims to create sustainable change and promote healthier lifestyles across the state.

TSET FOOD SYSTEMS IMPACT GRANTS

ADVANCING RESEARCH

Biomedical research is vibrant in Oklahoma and TSET dollars are part of priming and sustaining the work.

TSET has been a consistent supporter of the OU Health Stephenson Cancer Center (SCC). The center, which offers cancer treatment to Oklahomans across the state, achieved National Cancer Institute (NCI) designation in 2018 and continues to advance its work to prevent and reduce risk factors for cancer, pioneer new treatments, and provide hope to Oklahomans facing a cancer diagnosis.

TSET's funding of the Phase 1 Clinical Trials Program has been top in the nation for participation rate and is among the top 10 Phase 1 centers in the nation. The trials provide hope to cancer patients who may have exhausted other cancer therapy. Work at SCC has led to eight new FDA-approved cancer drugs.

Research is key to understanding risk factors for cancer and pushing for innovation in helping people quit smoking. The TSET Health Promotion Research Center works to reduce the burden of disease by addressing modifiable health risk factors through research, new intervention methods, and sharing those finding.

High impact publications explore the effectiveness of managing tobacco or substance abuse cravings with mobile technology or explores ways to make tobacco cessation more effective especially in populations that have higher than average cancer diagnosis and mortality rates. Ninety-three studies have used

Dr. Robert Mannel is CEO of the OU Health Stephenson Cancer Center.

In 2014, TSET awarded a grant for more than $14 million to the Oklahoma Center for Adult Stem Cell Research.

The OU Health Stephenson Cancer Center has been a major recipient of TSET grants.

Phase 1 trials at the OU Health Stephenson Cancer Center are the first time that treatment protocols are used outside of the laboratory.

the mobile-health platform, and more than 2,300 Oklahomans have participated in research studies. The TSET Health Promotion Research Center is also expanding its work into supporting physical activity and nutrition.

Understanding how cells work is also key to developing screenings and innovative treatment. TSET's funding to the Oklahoma Center for Adult Stem Cell Research, collaboratively governed by a steering committee that includes members from Oklahoma State University, OU Health Sciences Center, and the Oklahoma Medical Research Foundation has helped bring in more than $338 million in additional private and federal grants. Many of the grants focus on understanding the risk factors for cancer and obesity.

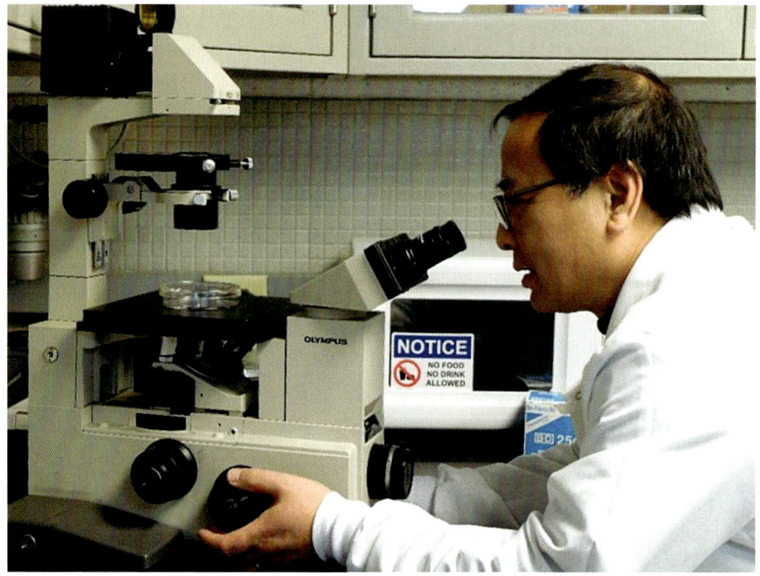

TSET considers research as a key component of fighting cancer in the future as researchers find more about risk factors and treatment.

CHAPTER FIFTEEN

A VISION FOR THE FUTURE

TSET is a trust for the people of Oklahoma. For a quarter of a century, TSET has been the primary funder of prevention and health improvement in the state. The structure of the endowment ensures there will always be funding for health improvement. The agency is poised to continue the work with new funding opportunities and innovative community grant programs.

As the agency looks to the future with a steady track record behind it, there are still opportunities for growth and improvement in Oklahoma's health.

In 2018, the TSET Board of Directors, approved a bold resolution that recommended 12 actions to cut adult smoking in half by 2028. The measure called for changes in law to reduce secondhand smoke exposure, ban menthol and other flavored tobacco products, strengthen laws to prevent underage Oklahomans from accessing tobacco products, license of vapor retailers, and tax vapor products, as well as reduce the density tobacco retailers in Oklahoma neighborhoods.

"TSET has been working on these challenges for 20 years and we continue to strongly believe that it is our mission now and, in the future, to create a healthier Oklahoma," said 2020 Board Chairman Bruce Benjamin.

As TSET celebrates its 25th anniversary, many of these policy changes remain elusive. Tobacco use remains the leading cause of preventable death. In 2024, Oklahoma's rate of adult vaping outpaced the national average.

"Big Tobacco is very supportive of Oklahoma laws that make it easier for adults to vape and keep them addicted. Vaping is Big Tobacco's latest trick," TSET Executive Director Bisbee said.

TSET Executive Director Julie Bisbee visits with students at the Youth Action for Health Leadership (YAHL) Leadership Team Summit in 2024. Students from across the state gather each summer in Oklahoma City to learn how to lead health-promoting change in their schools and communities.

As TSET looks to the future, preventing youth from starting tobacco use will continue to be an area of investment. Over the years, TSET has worked across the state to support healthy choices for young people, such as nutritious eating, moving more and staying tobacco and vape free.

One program building a healthier tomorrow is the Youth Action for Health Leadership (YAHL). This program partners with schools, clubs, and community organizations to educate and advocate for change, whether that's working to improve the health environment of school districts and communities or educating on the benefits of strong laws at the State Capitol.

INNOVATION AND CONTINUOUS IMPROVEMENT

A guiding principle at TSET is ensuring the work is grounded in outcomes and follows new and emerging research. This key tenant helps TSET continue to be a national leader for preventing and reducing tobacco use and improving health outcomes. While change may be slow given the adversity Oklahoma faces—high rate of poverty, lower levels of post high school education, and other disparities—TSET and its partners will continue to push for pioneering ways to support Oklahomans.

"We have a duty to innovate, test new strategies and programs for reducing the toll of tobacco and improving health," Bisbee said. "Oklahoma continues to be the proving ground for innovative approaches to help people live healthier lives. It's imperative that we continue to challenge ourselves to push for improved health outcomes."

To foster innovation, TSET's Board of Directors has consistently invested in preventing and reducing the risk factors for cancer, as well as meeting its Constitutional mission to support the state's cancer center.

"Our goal . . . is not to just treat patients but improve outcomes and ultimately, cure, this terrible disease," Dr. Robert Mannel, director of Stephenson Cancer Center wrote. "We do this through research and TSET has been a critical partner."

A TSET print ad distinguishes between sacred tobacco and the campaign of Big Tobacco to hook Native American youth.

Oklahoma has the fourth-highest cancer death rate among all states, with higher rates of death among Native Americans, African Americans, and residents of rural areas. Stephenson Cancer Center is the state's only National Cancer Institute-designated cancer center and continues to push for advances. SCC has emerged as a national leader in enrolling patients in trials for new treatments and medications.

Looking to the future, SCC is well positioned to seek the additional distinction of becoming an NCI Comprehensive Cancer Center. With this distinction, work will also focus on improving cancer treatment, increasing access to clinical trials, increasing awareness of cancer risks, and screening at earlier stages.

In addition to advances in prevention, research, and training, the TSET Board of Directors has committed to increasing grants across the state for high impact work. Pockets of rural Oklahoma continue to have higher than average rates of tobacco use, obesity, cancer, and cardiovascular disease. TSET will continue to focus on partnerships, grants and programs that seek to close the gap on health improvement.

"Making best practices and evidence-based programs are the cornerstone of the agency's funding strategy," said Jonás Mata, a program architect at TSET with 20 years at the agency. "We consistently remain true throughout the years to addressing our mission, constitutional mandates, and financial stewardship."

With a strong record of success and a dedication to honor the purpose of the the endowment, TSET's future path remains clear: Improve the health of Oklahomans for generations to come.

In recent years, TSET has opened grant opportunities funding new and emerging programs and projects to improve health.

As part of its funding opportunity to increase walkability and access to physical activity, TSET grants have helped to create destinations for outdoor activity and master plans for sidewalks or spurred the development of a walkable downtown.

"People are connected to their communities, their families, and neighbors," Bisbee said. "Investing in spaces that help people gather, enjoy recreation or get active improve the quality of life in our towns and cities. Improving the health of Oklahomans is going to be a collaborative effort on all fronts, and we're excited to be a part of that."

While TSET has partnered with organizations and communities to create programs and amenities supporting healthy choices, changes in state law have not moved at the same pace.

Children and adults enjoy the TSET Shape Your Future garden at First Americans Museum in Oklahoma City.

Laws put in place by the tobacco industry in the 1980s limit the ability of local municipalities to enact ordinances stronger than state law that address:

1. Smoking in workplaces and public places
2. Tobacco advertising
3. Youth access to tobacco products

Research shows that neighborhoods with high tobacco retailer density and a high presence of tobacco advertisements have worse health outcomes. TSET and Oklahoma's community leaders are trying to create a healthier state, but lack a key tool at the local level. Survey data shows that an overwhelming majority of Oklahomans, 78%, support a law making all public places smokefree. Twenty-seven states allow local communities to pass ordinances to protect residents from second-hand smoke exposure. Smokefree laws not only protect people from secondhand smoke exposure, but these laws have also been shown to help people quit and help people smoke less. Reducing the harms of tobacco and secondhand smoke is important in reducing the number of Oklahomans diagnosed and killed by tobacco-related cancer.

In 2024, TSET Board Chairman Marshall Snipes said:

> We have much left to do, but the most important goal is to work with the legislature to pass a clean air act for the state and remove preemption from state law to allow cities and towns to pass stringent ordinances to reflect the people's wishes to severely limit the use of tobacco.

KEY DATES IN TSET HISTORY

1998 Master Settlement Agreement reached between 46 states and the tobacco industry

2000 Oklahoma is the first state to constitutionally protect its share of the tobacco settlement

2003 The Oklahoma Tobacco Hotline launched

2006 Communities of Excellence grants awarded in 17 counties

2009 TSET's first research grant awarded

2011 For the first time in history, Oklahoma has more *former* smokers than *present* smokers

2018 TSET-funded OU Health Stephenson Cancer Center achieves National Cancer Institute designation

2019 Youth smoking drops to single digits

2020 State Question 814, which seeks to reduce the annual Master Settlement Agreement contribution to the endowment, is rejected by voters in all 77 counties

2023 Adult smoking is at an all-time low

2024 One billion fewer cigarette packs were sold from 2001-2024 because of the reduction in the smoking rate

TSET Executive Director Julie Bisbee, front, with TSET staff at the Oklahoma State Capitol.

CURRENT BOARD MEMBERS AND STAFF

2024-2025 BOARD MEMBERS

KEN ROWE, CHAIRMAN

JENNIFER NEEDHAM, VICE CHAIRMAN

JACK ALLEN

BRUCE BENJAMIN

AARON HARMON

MARSHALL SNIPES

RUNAKO WHITTAKER, MD

2024-2025 STAFF

NATALIA ARBELAEZ

CANDICE BACON

KELLI BRODERSEN

LESTER BROWN

TRISH BRYANT

SAMUEL CARRILLO

SARAH CARSON

BRITT CHAPMAN

AMANDA CRIBBS

JESSICA DAVIS

ANGELA DALY

LAUREN CARTER FORD

KRYSTAL GEORGE

CHASE HARVICK

KAYE JAMES

DYLAN JASNA

BRIAN JEPSEN

THOMAS LARSON

SHAUN LAWRENCE

SARA LOW

TONIA LOWREY

LAURA MATLOCK

JONÁS OSIO MATA

JAMIE MCDANIEL

KELSEY NATION

BRITTANY NEWMAN

JADE OWEN

KELLY PARKER

SJONNA PAULSON

TERRY ROUSEY

KIRA SWITZER

J. LANCE THOMAS

DAWN THIMMIG

DENA TROSKY

JAME TYREE

ANDREW UNDERKOFFLER

TAYLOR VERKLER

EDDIE WITHERS

CAILIN WRIGHT

SUSAN YINGLING

EXECUTIVE DIRECTORS OF TSET

JULIE BISBEE, 2019-CURRENT

JOHN WOODS, NOVEMBER 2016-2018

TRACEY STRADER, 2002-JANUARY 2017

PAST BOARD MEMBERS OF TSET

MARVIN APPLE
SUSAN WALTERS BIZE
DONALD COOPER, MD
TRACY FOOR
GEORGE FOSTER, OD
SUSANNA GATTONI
JIM GEBHART
JOHN KENNEDY
CASEY KILLBLANE
CURTIS KNOLES
BILL LISSAU
BRIAN MADDY
ROBERT MCCAFFREE, MD
DON MILLICAN
LISA NOWLIN, DDS
SUZANNE OLIVE, MD
MICHELLE STEPHENS

PAST CHAIRMAN OF TSET

TERMS ARE NOVEMBER TO NOVEMBER

ROBERT MCCAFFREE 2001-2003, 2005-2006
SUSAN WALTERS BIZE 2003-2005
KEN ROWE 2006-2008; 2012-2013; 2024-PRESENT
CASEY KILLBLANE 2008-2010; 2012-2014
JIM GEBHART 2014-2016
DON MILLICAN 2016-2018
MICHELLE STEPHENS 2020-2022
MARSHALL SNIPES 2022-2024

TSET BOARD OF INVESTORS

CHAIRED BY STATE TREASURER TODD RUSS, 2023-PRESENT

AARON ACKERMAN
BRENDA BOLANDER
TODD DOBSON
TYSON GOETZ
DAVID HINKLE
MIKE MAYHALL
DEBORAH MUEGGENBORG
DONALD PAPE
DAVID RAINBOLT
WILLIAM SCHONACHER
STEVE TINSLEY
PHIL TOHLEN
R. SCOTT VAUGHN
JOHN WALDO
JIMMY WILLIAMS

TSET GRANTEES

JULY 1, 2023-JUNE 30, 2024

BUILT ENVIRONMENT AND INNOVATIONS GRANTS

CITY OF MCALESTER

CITY OF PAULS VALLEY

CITY OF PAULS VALLEY

CITY OF PRYOR CREEK

CITY OF SEMINOLE

CITY OF SEMINOLE

CITY OF TISHOMINGO

CUSHING PUBLIC SCHOOLS

EASTERN OKLAHOMA STATE COLLEGE

HEALTHY SCHOOLS OKLAHOMA - BETHANY CHILDREN'S HEALTH CENTER

OKLAHOMA STATE UNIVERSITY - OKC

OKLAHOMA STATE UNIVERSITY WASTEWATER

RIVERSPOR 1, 20T FOUNDATION

THE BOTANIC GARDEN AT OSU

TOWN OF FORT COBB

TOWN OF LOCUST GROVE

TOWN OF WESTVILLE

CONFERENCE SPONSORSHIPS

ACTIVATE OKLAHOMA INC.

COALITION OF OKLAHOMA BREASTFEEDING ADVOCATES

JACKSON COUNTY COMMUNITY HEALTH ACTION TEAM

MYRIAD GARDENS FOUNDATION

NATIONAL ASSOCIATION OF SOCIAL WORKERS -OKLAHOMA

OKLAHOMA ASSOCIATION OF COMMUNITY ACTION AGENCIES

OKLAHOMA ASSOCIATION OF HEALTH, PHYSICAL EDUCATION, RECREATION, AND DANCE

OKLAHOMA BIKE SUMMIT, INC.

OKLAHOMA CARING FOUNDATION, INC.

OKLAHOMA DEPARTMENT OF VETERAN AFFAIRS

OKLAHOMA HEALTHY AGING INITIATIVE

OKLAHOMA MUSEUM ASSOCIATION

OKLAHOMA PUBLIC HEALTH ASSOCIATION

RURAL HEALTH ASSOCIATION OF OKLAHOMA

SCHOOL NURSE ORGANIZATION OF OKLAHOMA

SOARING EAGLE'S YOUTH AND FAMILY SERVICES

THE OKLAHOMA INSTITUTE FOR CHILD ADVOCACY

UNIVERSITY OF OKLAHOMA HEALTH SCIENCES CENTER LOCAL AGRICULTURE SUMMIT

WOMEN HELPING OTHER WOMEN ORGANIZATION

DISCOVERY GRANTS

CITY OF SALLISAW

LIFE SENIOR SERVICES

NEWVIEW OKLAHOMA

OKLAHOMA SENIOR GAMES

OKLAHOMA STATE UNIVERSITY

UNIVERSITY OF OKLAHOMA HEALTH SCIENCES CENTER - SAVING TINY SOONERS

RIVER PARKS FOUNDATION

FOOD SYSTEMS IMPACT GRANTS

HUNGER FREE OKLAHOMA

HEALTH COMMUNICATION

OKLAHOMA HEALTH CARE AUTHORITY - SOONERQUIT PROGRAM

RESCUE - YOUTH MEDIA AND MARKETING CAMPAIGN

VI MARKETING AND BRANDING — ADULT-FOCUSED CAMPAIGNS AND OKLAHOMA TOBACCO HELPLINE PROMOTION

HEALTH EDUCATION PARTNERSHIP

OKLAHOMA STATE DEPARTMENT OF EDUCATION

HEALTHY COMMUNITIES INCENTIVE GRANTS

CITY OF CHICKASHA

CITY OF DEL CITY

TOWN OF HULBERT

TOWN OF LANGLEY

CITY OF PRAGUE

CITY OF PURCELL

CITY OF SPENCER

CITY OF STILWELL

TOWN OF TAMAHA

CITY OF TUTTLE

CITY OF WILBURTON

HEALTHY SCHOOLS INCENTIVE GRANTS

ALEX PUBLIC SCHOOLS

ALTUS EARLY CHILDHOOD CENTER

ALTUS ELEMENTARY SCHOOL

ALTUS HIGH SCHOOL

ALTUS INTERMEDIATE SCHOOL

ALTUS JUNIOR HIGH

ALTUS PRIMARY SCHOOL

BEN FRANKLIN: 6TH AND 7TH GRADE ACADEMY (MUSKOGEE)

CHARTER OAK ELEMENTARY SCHOOL (GUTHRIE)

COMANCHE MIDDLE SCHOOL

DEER CREEK PUBLIC SCHOOLS

DEER CREEK ELEMENTARY SCHOOL

ENID PUBLIC SCHOOLS

FINLEY-REESE ELEMENTARY (WRIGHT CITY)

JENKS MIDDLE SCHOOL

L MENDEL RIVERS ELEMENTARY SCHOOL (ALTUS)

LAWTON PUBLIC SCHOOLS

LEFLORE PUBLIC SCHOOLS

LINDSAY PUBLIC SCHOOLS

MCLOUD PUBLIC SCHOOLS

MEEKER PUBLIC SCHOOLS

MORRISON ELEMENTARY SCHOOL

MORRISON HIGH SCHOOL

MORRISON MIDDLE SCHOOL

NORTH ROCK CREEK HIGH SCHOOL

OKLAHOMA SCHOOL FOR THE BLIND

OKTAHA ELEMENTARY SCHOOL

PERSHING ELEMENTARY SCHOOL (MUSKOGEE)

RED OAK PUBLIC SCHOOLS

SAND SPRINGS PUBLIC SCHOOLS

STILLWATER HIGH SCHOOL (LINCOLN ACADEMY)

STILLWATER JUNIOR HIGH SCHOOL

STILWELL HIGH SCHOOL

STILWELL MIDDLE SCHOOL

STRINGTOWN PUBLIC SCHOOLS

TURKEY FORD PUBLIC SCHOOLS

TUSKAHOMA PUBLIC SCHOOLS

TSET HEALTHY LIVING PROGRAM

CANADIAN COUNTY HEALTH DEPARTMENT

CHEROKEE COUNTY HEALTH SERVICES COUNCIL

CHEROKEE NATION PUBIC HEALTH (SERVING ADAIR COUNTY)

COMANCHE COUNTY MEMORIAL HOSPITAL

GATEWAY TO PREVENTION AND RECOVERY INC. (SERVING POTTAWATOMIE COUNTY)

GRAND NATION INC. (SERVING CRAIG COUNTY)

GREAT PLAINS YOUTH AND FAMILY SERVICES (SERVING CADDO AND KIOWA COUNTIES)

KI BOIS COMMUNITY ACTION FOUNDATION INC. (SERVING HASKELL COUNTY)

KINGFISHER COUNTY HEALTH DEPARTMENT (SERVING BLAINE AND KINGFISHER COUNTIES)

LEFLORE COUNTY YOUTH SERVICES, INC.

LINCOLN COUNTY HEALTH DEPARTMENT

MAYES COUNTY HOPE COALITION

MCCLAIN-GARVIN COUNTY YOUTH & FAMILY CENTER (SERVING GARVIN COUNTY) (DBA- FRONTLINE FAMILY SOLUTIONS)

MUSKOGEE COUNTY HEALTH DEPARTMENT

NORMAN REGIONAL HEALTH SYSTEM (SERVING CLEVELAND COUNTY)

NORMAN REGIONAL HEALTH SYSTEM (SERVING GRADY COUNTY)

NORMAN REGIONAL HEALTH SYSTEM (SERVING MCCLAIN COUNTY)

NOWATA CAN INC. (SERVING NOWATA COUNTY)

OKLAHOMA CITY-COUNTY HEALTH DEPARTMENT

OKLAHOMA STATE UNIVERSITY (SERVING CREEK COUNTY)

OKLAHOMA STATE UNIVERSITY (SERVING KAY COUNTY)

OKLAHOMA STATE UNIVERSITY (SERVING PAYNE COUNTY)

PEOPLE INC. (SERVING SEQUOYAH COUNTY)

ROCMND LLC- ROCMND AREA YOUTH SERVICES (SERVING DELAWARE COUNTY)

ROGERS COUNTY VOLUNTEERS FOR YOUTH INC.

RURAL HEALTH PROJECTS INC. (SERVING GARFIELD COUNTY)

TULSA CITY-COUNTY HEALTH DEPARTMENT

WICHITA MOUNTAINS PREVENTION NETWORK INC. (SERVING CARTER COUNTY)

HEALTH SYSTEMS INITIATIVES & EMERGING OPPORTUNITIES

HEALTH CARE WORKFORCE TRAINING COMMISSION

OKLAHOMA DEPARTMENT OF MENTAL HEALTH AND SUBSTANCE ABUSE - PREVENTION SERVICES

OKLAHOMA HEALTH CARE AUTHORITY - SOONERQUIT PROVIDER ENGAGEMENT

OKLAHOMA HOSPITAL ASSOCIATION

OKLAHOMA STATE UNIVERSITY CENTER FOR HEALTH SCIENCES - PROJECT ECHO

OKLAHOMA STATE UNIVERSITY - CHS MEDICAL RESIDENCIES

UNIVERSITY OF OKLAHOMA HEALTH SCIENCES CENTER - OK LUNG SCAN

UNIVERSITY OF OKLAHOMA HEALTH SCIENCES CENTER - OKLAHOMA ADULT TOBACCO SURVEY

OKLAHOMA TOBACCO HELPLINE

UNIVERSITY OF OKLAHOMA HEALTH SCIENCES CENTER – HELPLINE OVERSIGHT

UNIVERSITY OF OKLAHOMA HEALTH SCIENCES CENTER – HELPLINE CALLER SERVICES PROVIDED BY RVO

PROGRAM EVALUATION

UNIVERSITY OF OKLAHOMA HEALTH SCIENCES CENTER - HUDSON COLLEGE OF PUBLIC HEALTH

RESEARCH

OKLAHOMA MEDICAL RESEARCH FOUNDATION - OKLAHOMA CENTER FOR ADULT STEM CELL RESEARCH

TSET HEALTH PROMOTION RESEARCH CENTER

TSET CANCER RESEARCH PROGRAM AT OU HEALTH STEPHENSON CANCER CENTER

SE OKLAHOMA TARGETED ACHIEVEMENT GRANTS

KI BOIS PITTSBURG COUNTY

TECHNICAL ASSISTANCE, TRAINING AND CONSULTING

BERRYDUNN MCNEIL & PARKER

CHANGELAB SOLUTIONS

EMORY UNIVERSITY

ONSIDE PARTNERS

TIGRIS SOLUTIONS, LLC

TSET SUCCESSFUL FUTURES GRANTS

OKLAHOMA ASSOCIATION OF YOUTH SERVICES

YOUTH PROGRAMS

RESCUE - YOUTH ADVOCACY AND EDUCATION

THE CONSTITUTIONAL AMENDMENT

Article 10, Section 40 of the Oklahoma Constitution

A. There is hereby created a trust fund to be known as the " Tobacco Settlement Endowment Trust Fund". The trust fund principal shall consist of the portion of monies which are received by the State of Oklahoma on or after July 1, 2001, pursuant to any settlement with or judgment against any tobacco company or companies as provided by subsection B of this section, and any other monies that may be appropriated or otherwise directed to the trust fund by the Legislature.

B. 1. Deposits into the trust fund from monies which are received by the State of Oklahoma pursuant to any settlement with or judgment against any tobacco company or companies shall be based on the following schedule:

Fiscal Year	Minimum Percentage of Payments
Ending June 30, 2002	50%
Ending June 30, 2003	55%
Ending June 30, 2004	60%
Ending June 30, 2005	65%
Ending June 30, 2006	70%
Ending June 30, 2007	75%

2. Deposits into the trust fund in subsequent fiscal years shall never be less than seventy-five percent (75%) of the payments.

3. The monies received by the State of Oklahoma pursuant to any settlement with or judgment against any tobacco company or companies after June 30, 2001, not deposited into the trust fund as provided in this section, shall be deposited into a special fund established by the Legislature solely for the purpose of receiving the payments; provided, the Legislature may, by law, direct a certain portion of such monies to the Office of the Attorney General. The special fund shall be subject to legislative appropriations.

C. There is hereby created the Board of Investors of the Tobacco Settlement Endowment Trust Fund. The Board of Investors shall have the duty of investing monies in the trust fund, subject to restrictions and limitations provided by law for and in accordance with laws applicable to the investment of monies in state retirement funds.

The Board of Investors shall consist of five (5) members as follows:

1. The State Treasurer who shall be the chair;
2. An appointee of the Governor;
3. An appointee of the Speaker of the House of Representatives;
4. An appointee of the President Pro Tempore of the Senate; and
5. An appointee of the State Auditor and Inspector.

The initial appointees shall serve staggered terms of office as provided for by law. Thereafter, appointees shall serve four-year terms of office. No more than two appointees shall be appointed from any single congressional district. All appointed members shall have demonstrated expertise in public or private investment funds management.

D. There is hereby created the Board of Directors of the Tobacco Settlement Endowment Trust Fund. The Board of Directors shall consist of seven (7) members, one appointed by each of the following appointing authorities:

1. The Governor;
2. The President Pro Tempore of the Senate;
3. The Speaker of the House of Representatives;
4. The Attorney General;
5. The State Treasurer;
6. The State Auditor and Inspector; and
7. The State Superintendent of Public Instruction.

The initial appointed members shall serve staggered terms of office as provided for by law. Thereafter, the appointed members of the Board of Directors shall serve seven-year terms of office. At least one appointee shall be appointed from each congressional district, and not more than two appointees shall be appointed from any single congressional district. Not more than four appointees shall be members of the same political party. An appointee shall have been a member of the political party to which the appointee belongs for at least one (1) year prior to the date of appointment. Appointees shall have demonstrated expertise in public or private health care or programs related to or for the benefit of children or senior adults.

The Board of Directors shall meet at least one time each calendar quarter.

E. Earnings from the trust fund, including but not limited to interest, dividends, and realized capital gains from investments of the trust fund shall be expended as provided in subsection F of this section for the following purposes:

1. Clinical and basic research and treatment efforts in Oklahoma for the purpose of enhancing efforts to prevent and combat cancer and other tobacco-related diseases;
2. Cost-effective tobacco prevention and cessation programs;
3. Programs other than those specified in paragraph 1 of this subsection designed to maintain or improve the health of Oklahomans or to enhance the provision of health care services to Oklahomans, with particular emphasis on such programs for children;
4. Programs and services for the benefit of the children of Oklahoma, with particular emphasis on common and higher education, before- and after-school and pre-school programs, substance abuse prevention and treatment programs and other programs and services designed to improve the health and quality of life of children;
5. Programs designed to enhance the health and well-being of senior adults; and
6. Authorized administrative expenses of the Office of the State Treasurer and the Board of Directors.

F. Each fiscal year, the Board of Directors may expend the amount of earnings which actually accrued to the trust fund during the preceding fiscal year. Any amount not so expended shall remain in the trust fund. The Board shall direct specific expenditures to be made for the purposes specified in subsection E of this section.

G. The Legislature may enact laws to further implement the provisions of this section.

OPINION OF THE ATTORNEY GENERAL OF OKLAHOMA

2007 AG 30, SEPTERMBER 20, 2007

1. **May the Oklahoma Legislature lawfully enact legislation directing expenditures from the earnings of the Oklahoma Tobacco Settlement Endowment Trust Fund ("Trust Fund") for specific programs or purposes?**

2. **May the Legislature lawfully enact legislation directing the Board of Directors of the Trust Fund to make expenditures from the Trust Fund for specific programs or purposes?**

¶1 In 2000, the citizens of the State of Oklahoma voted to create the Tobacco Settlement Endowment Trust Fund ("Trust Fund"). *See* 2000 Okla. Sess. Laws ch. 249, § 1 (codified at Okla. Const. art. X, § 40). The Trust Fund is made up of revenues received by the State of Oklahoma "pursuant to any settlement with or judgment against any tobacco company or companies . . . and any other monies that may be appropriated or otherwise directed to the trust fund by the Legislature." Okla. Const. art. X, § 40(A). Section 40(B) of Article X provides that deposits into the Trust Fund from monies received by the State of Oklahoma shall be based on the following schedule:

Fiscal Year	Minimum Percentage of Payments
Ending June 30, 2002	50%
Ending June 30, 2003	55%
Ending June 30, 2004	60%
Ending June 30, 2005	65%
Ending June 30, 2006	70%
Ending June 30, 2007	75%

Id. In subsequent fiscal years, deposits shall never be less than seventy-five percent (75%) of the payments. Okla. Const. art. X, § 40(B)(2). Monies which are not deposited into the Trust Fund are to be deposited into a special fund established by the Legislature for the purpose of receiving the payments. Okla. Const. art. X, § 40(B)(3). The Constitution gives the Legislature authority to appropriate monies from this special fund. *Id.*

¶2 The Constitution creates a Board of Investors and a Board of Directors of the Trust Fund and prescribes duties for each board. Okla. Const. art. X, § 40(C),(D). The Constitution specifically gives the Legislature the power to enact legislation to implement the constitutional provisions. Okla. Const. art. X § 40(G).

¶3 You ask whether the Legislature may lawfully enact legislation directing expenditures from the earnings from the Trust Fund for specific programs or purposes, and whether the Legislature may lawfully enact legislation directing the Board of Directors of the Trust Fund to make expenditures from the Trust Fund for specific programs or purposes. These expenditures from the earnings of the Trust Fund are separate from monies constitutionally given to the Legislature to appropriate into the special legislative fund.

¶4 The purposes for which the earnings from the Trust Fund are to be spent are set forth in the Constitution, which provides that the Board of Directors may expend trust fund earnings on the following programs:

1. Clinical and basic research and treatment efforts in Oklahoma for the purpose of enhancing efforts to prevent and combat cancer and other tobacco-related diseases;

2. Cost-effective tobacco prevention and cessation programs;

3. Programs other than those specified in paragraph 1 of this subsection designed to maintain or improve the health of Oklahomans or to enhance the provision of health care services to Oklahomans, with particular emphasis on such programs for children;

4. Programs and services for the benefit of the children of Oklahoma, with particular emphasis on common and higher education, before- and after-school and pre-school programs, substance abuse prevention and treatment programs and other programs and services designed to improve the health and quality of life of children;

5. Programs designed to enhance the health and well-being of senior adults; and

6. Authorized administrative expenses of the Office of the State Treasurer and the Board of Directors.

   Okla. Const. art. X, § 40(E). Subsection F of Section 40 of Article X of the Constitution vests the authority to direct specific expenditures with the Board of Directors. That provision states:

F. Each fiscal year, ***the Board of Directors*** may expend the amount of earnings which actually accrued to the trust fund during the preceding fiscal year. Any amount not so expended shall remain in the trust fund. ***The Board shall direct specific expenditures to be made for the purposes specified in subsection E of this section.***

Id. (emphasis added).

¶5 "A constitutional provision is to be applied to give effect to the intent of the people voting on it." *In re Protest Against the Tax Levy*, 959 P.2d 580, 582 (Okla. 1998). "The intent is determined by the provision itself, and where unambiguous, courts are not at liberty to search beyond the instrument for its meaning." *Id.* The intent of the constitutional provision from the plain, unambiguous language of the Constitution is that: (1) the Board of Directors directs the specific expenditures to be made from the Trust Fund, and (2) the expenditures must be made for the purposes set forth in subsection E.

¶6 In 2001, the Oklahoma Legislature created the Tobacco Settlement Endowment Trust Fund Act ("Act") to implement the constitutional provision. *See* 2001 Okla. Sess. Laws ch. 274 (codified at 62 O.S. 2001, §§ 2301 - 2310). The Act states its purpose is to "further implement the provisions of Section 40 of Article X of the Oklahoma Constitution that," among other things, "[a]uthorize[] the Board of Directors of the [Trust Fund] to expend trust fund earnings for specific purposes." 62 O.S. 2001, § 2302. Regarding the Legislature's power to implement constitutional provisions, the Oklahoma Supreme Court stated:

Whether a provision of a Constitution be self-executing or not be self-executing, supplemental legislation facilitating the carrying into effect of the rights secured, and safeguarding the rights against abuses, may be desirable; but such legislation must be in harmony with the spirit of the Constitution and must not curtail the rights reserved or exceed the limitations specified.

In re Initiative Petition No. 281 v. Rogers, 434 P.2d 941, 952 (Okla. 1967).

¶7 Additionally, the Oklahoma Supreme Court has said that "[w]hile the law-making power of the Legislature is supreme within its proper sphere, that power may be restricted and limited by constitutional provisions." *Bd. of Regents v. Baker*, 638 P.2d 464, 466 (Okla. 1981). "Limitations on legislative authority may be implied as well as expressed in the Constitution." *Id.*

¶8 The Constitution specifically grants the Board of Directors the power to direct the expenditures to be made from the earnings of the Trust Fund. Okla. Const. art. X, § 40(F). This positive delegation of power by the Constitution to the Board of Directors implies a negation of its exercise by any other officer or department. *Baker*, 638 P.2d at 466. Legislation which would grant the Legislature the power to direct the expenditures from the Trust Fund or which would allow the Legislature to direct the Board of Directors to spend the earnings from the Trust Fund for specific programs or purposes, would be inconsistent with the Constitution as it would restrict the constitutional power of the Board of Directors.

¶9 Therefore, to answer your question, any legislation that directs certain expenditures to be made from the earnings of the Trust Fund or which directs the Board of Directors to make certain expenditures from the earnings of the Trust Fund would be inconsistent with the Oklahoma Constitution. Even if the expenditures in question are those which fall within the categories listed in subsection E of Okla. Const. art. X, § 40, legislation which directs that the expenditures be made or which directs the Board of Directors to make them would be inconsistent with the Constitution. Under the unambiguous terms of the Constitution, it is the responsibility of the Board of Directors rather than the Legislature to determine the expenditures to be made from the Trust Fund earnings.

¶10 It is, therefore, the official Opinion of the Attorney General that:

The Oklahoma Constitution Article X, Section 40 governs the Tobacco Settlement Endowment Trust Fund and provides that the Board of Directors of the Trust Fund is responsible for directing the expenditure of earnings from the Trust Fund. Any legislation which directs expenditures to be made from the Trust Fund for specific programs or purposes or which directs the Board of Directors to make expenditures from the Trust Fund for specific programs or purposes would be inconsistent with the Oklahoma Constitution.

W.A. DREW EDMONDSON
Attorney General of Oklahoma

SANDRA D. RINEHART
Senior Assistant Attorney General

BIBLIOGRAPHY

BOOKS

Bahamondes, Marcia Erazo and Kjersti Nes. *Cigarette Smoking: Health Effects and Challenges for Tobacco Control,* (New York: Nova Science Publishing, Inc., 2017)

Benson, Peter. *Tobacco Capitalism: Growers, Migrant Workers, and the Changing face of a Global Industry,* (Princeton, New Jersey: Princeton University Press, 2011)

Breen, T.H. *Tobacco Culture: The Mentality of the Great Tidewater Planters on the Eve of the Revolution,* (Princeton, New Jersey: Princeton University Press, 1987)

Brewer, Judson and Jon Kabat-Zinn. *The Craving Mind,* (New Haven, Connecticut: Yale University Press, 2018)

Burns, Eric. *The Smoke of the Gods: A Social History of Tobacco,* (Philadelphia: Temple University Press, 2006)

Carr, Allen. *The Easy Way to Stop Smoking,* (Richmond, Virgina: Clarity Marketing USA LLC, 2011)

Gately, Iain. *Tobacco: A Cultural History of How an Exotic Plant Seduced Civilization,* (New York: Grove Press, 2007)

Givel, Michael S. and Andrew L. Spivak. *Heartland Tobacco War,* (Lanham, Maryland: Lexington Books, 2013)

Goodin, Robert E. *No Smoking: The Ethical Issues,* (Chicago: University of Chicago Press, 1990)

Goodman, Jordan. *Tobacco in History,* (Milton Park, UK: Routledge, 1993)

Gottsegen, Jack Jacob. *Tobacco: A Study of Its Consumption in the United States,* (Lanham, Maryland: Pitman Publishing Company, 1940)

Harris, Ralph and Judith Hatton. *Murder a Cigarette,* (London: Duckworth, 1998)

Haustein, Knut-Olaf and David Groneberg. *Tobacco or Health? Physiological and Social Damage Caused by Tobacco Smoking,* (New York: Springer Publishing Co., 2002)

Heyes, Eileen. *Tobacco USA: the Industry Behind the Smoke Curtain,* (Minneapolis, Minnesota: Twenty First Century Books, 1999)

Hoots, Gene, *Going Down Tobacco Road: R.J. Reynolds' Tobacco Empire: The Gold Leaf and North Carolina,* (Chicago: Encore Consulting Inc., 2020)

Houston, T.P., ed. *Tobacco Use: An American Crisis, Final Conference Report and Recommendations from America's Health Community,* (Washington, DC: American Medical Association, 1993.

Hughes, Jason. *Learning to Smoke: Tobacco Use in the West,* (Chicago: University of Chicago Press, 2003)

Jacobson, Peter, et al. *Combating Teen Smoking: Research and Policy Strategies,* (Ann Arbor, Michigan: University of Michigan Press, 2001)

Jacobson, Peter, J. Wasserman, and K. Raube. *The Political Evolution of Anti-Smoking Legislation,* (Santa Monica, California: Rand Corporation, 1992)

Jason, Leonard A. and Steven B. Pakorny. *Preventing Youth Access to Tobacco,* (Milton Park, UK: Routledge, 2002)

Klein, Richard. *Cigarettes Are Sublime,* (Durham, North Carolina: Duke University Press, 1993)

Kluger, Richard. *Ashes to Ashes,* (New York: Vintage Books, 1997)

Loddenkemper, M. Kreuter, ed. *The Tobacco Epidemic,* (Basel, Switzerland: Karger Publishers, 1997)

Milov, Sarah. *The Cigarette: A Political History,* (Cambridge, Massachusetts: Harvard University Press, 2019)

Oreskes, Naomi and Erik M. Conway. *Merchants of Doubt: How a handful of scientists obscured the truth on issues from tobacco to global warming,* (New York, Bloomsbury Publishing USA, 2011)

Pampel, Fred C. *Tobacco Industry and Smoking,* (New York: Facts of File, Inc., 2009)

Pertschuk, Michael. *Smoke In Their Eyes,* (Nashville: University of Tennessee Press, 2001)

Pertschuk, Michael and A. Erickson. *Smoke Fighting: A Smoking Control Movement Building Guide,* (Atlanta, Georgia: American Cancer Society, 1989)

Proctor, R.N. *Cancer Wars,* (New York: Basic Books, 1995)

Rafferty, Sean M. *Smoking & Culture,* (Nashville: University of Tennessee Press, 2004)

Robert, Joseph C. *The Story of Tobacco in America,* (Whitefish, Montana: Kessinger Publishing LLC, 2007)

Robicsek, Francis. *The Smoking Gods: Tobacco in Maya Art, History, and Religion,* (Norman: University of Oklahoma Press, 1979)

Bonnie, R.J. and K.R. Stratton and R.B. Wallace, eds. *Ending the Tobacco Problem: A Blueprint for the Nation.* (Washington: National Academies Press; 2007)

Swanson, Hannah. *Tobacco Products: Regulation, Control, Taxes, and Exports,* (New York: Nova Science Publishers Inc., 2008)

Tatham, William. *An Historical and Practical Essay on the Culture and Commerce of Tobacco,* (London: Vernor and Hood/ Bensley, 1800)

Troyer, R.J. and G.E. Markle. *Cigarettes: The Battle Over Smoking,* (New Brunswick, New Jersey: Rutgers University Press, 1983)

Viscusi, W. Kip. *Smoke-Filled Rooms: A Postmorten on the Tobacco Deal,* (Chicago: University of Chicago Press, 2002)

Viscusi, W. Kip. *Smoking: Making the Risky Decision,* (New York: Oxford University Press, 1992)

Wagner, S. *Cigarette Country: Tobacco in American History and Politics,* (New York: Praeger, 1971)

Ward, J.W. and C. Warren. *Silent Victories: The History and Practice of Public Health in Twentieth-Century America,* (New York: Oxford University Press; 2007)

Wilbert, Johannes. *Tobacco and Shamanism in South America,* (New Haven, Connecticut: Yale University Press, 1993

Winter, Joseph C. *Tobacco Use by Native North Americans: Sacred Smoke and Silent Killer,* (Norman: University of Oklahoma Press, 2022)

Wolfson, Mark. *The Fight Against Big Tobacco,* (Milton Park, UK: Routledge, 2001)

RESEARCH

Department of Biostatistics and Epidemiology, Hudson College of Public Health, OUHSC. *Oklahoma Medicaid Savings Attributable to Smoking Cessation: An Analysis Prepared for the Oklahoma Tobacco Settlement Endowment Trust (TSET).* Oct. 17, 2024.

Matheny, D., TSET Health Promotion Research Center. *In Their Own Words: An Analysis of Internal Tobacco Industry Documents on Interference in Oklahoma laws,* 2020. Published by OU Health Stephenson Cancer Center.

Mushtaq, N. and L. Beebe, Department of Biostatistics and Epidemiology, Hudson College of Public Health, OUHSC, *Oklahoma Medicaid Savings Attributable to Smoking Cessation: An Analysis Prepared for the Oklahoma Tobacco Settlement Endowment Trust (TSET),* Oct. 20, 2021

MEDICAL JOURNALS AND WEBSITES THAT CONTAIN ARTICLES ON "TOBACCO SMOKING," "TOBACCO AND CANCER," AND "TOBACCO SETTLEMENT"

American Cancer Society, www.cancer.org

American Journal of Medicine, The, www.sciencedirect.com

American Journal of Preventive Medicine, www.ajpmonline.org

American Journal of Public Health, www.ajph.aphapublications.org

American Lung Association, www.action.lung.org

British Medical Journal, www.bmj.com

Campaign for Tobacco-free Kids, www.tobaccofreekids.org

Centers for Disease Control and Prevention, The, www.cdc.com

Journal of Applied Developmental Psychology, www.sciencedirect.org

Journal of Family Practice, www.mdedge.com

Journal of Pediatric Psychology, www.academic.oup.com

Journal of Social Service Research, www.rajpub.com

Journal of the American College of Cardiology, www.jacc.org

Journal of the American Dental Association, www.ada.org

Journal of the American Heart Association, www.ahajournals.org

Journal of the American Medical Association, www.jama.org

National Cancer Institute, www.cancer.gov

National Center for Chronic Disease Prevention and Health Promotion Office on Smoking and Health, pubmed.ncbi.nlm.nih.gov

National Institutes of Health, www.ncbi.nim.nih.gov

National Library of Medicine, www.nlm.com

Nature: Human Behavior, www.nature.com

New England Journal of Medicine, www.nejm.org

Profiles in Science, www.profiles.nlm.nih.gov

Publications and Reports of the Surgeon General of the United States, www.ncbi.nlm.nih.gov

Science News, www.sciencenews.org

Tobacco Control, www. tobaccocontrol.bmj.com

Truth Tobacco Industry Documents, www.industrydocuments.ucsf.edu /tobacco/docs

U.S. Department of Health and Human Services, www.hhs.gov

U.S. Food and Drug Administration, www.fda.gov

World Health Organization, www.who.int

Public Health Reports/Tobacco Use Among American Indians in Oklahoma, www.ncbi.nlm.nih.gov/pmc/

INDEX